Henry Edward Manning

The Reunion of Christendom

A Pastoral Letter to the Clergy

Henry Edward Manning

The Reunion of Christendom
A Pastoral Letter to the Clergy

ISBN/EAN: 9783744691673

Printed in Europe, USA, Canada, Australia, Japan

Cover: Foto ©Lupo / pixelio.de

More available books at **www.hansebooks.com**

THE REUNION OF CHRISTENDOM.

A PASTORAL LETTER TO THE CLERGY

ETC.

BY

HENRY EDWARD

ARCHBISHOP OF WESTMINSTER.

LONDON:
LONGMANS, GREEN, AND CO.
1866.

LONDON
PRINTED BY SPOTTISWOODE AND CO.
NEW-STREET SQUARE

REVEREND AND DEAR BRETHREN,—

In the Synod of the Diocese held on the 14th of December in last year, I published a Letter of the Supreme Congregation of the Holy Office, in reply to a communication of the Bishops of England relating to a society called an 'Association for Promoting the Unity of Christendom,' to which certain Catholics had become unwarily united. I made known to you also at the same time that the Holy Office had transmitted another document on the same subject, which it was my intention at a future time to communicate to the Clergy of the Diocese, together with certain instructions on the subject. This promise I will now fulfil.

It is not our practice in any official way to take cognizance of the affairs of those who are without, nor is there in the above-named Association any intrinsic importance to lead me to depart from our usual path. But special reasons induce me to do so, and they are the two documents which have been elicited from the supreme judicial authority of the Church, and the principles enunciated in them.

Inasmuch, Reverend and dear Brethren, as some of you may not be aware of the precise nature of the Association in question, I will begin with describing it; and that the description may be unimpeachable, it shall be given in the words of its own declaration. The founders and promoters of it announce it as follows:

'*Association for the Promotion of the Unity of Christendom.*

'An Association has been formed under the above title, to unite in a bond of intercessory prayer members both of the clergy and laity of the Roman Catholic, Greek, and Anglican communions. It is hoped and believed that many, however widely separated at present in their religious convictions, who deplore the grievous scandal to unbelievers, and the hindrance to the promotion of truth and holiness among Christians, caused by the unhappy divisions existing amongst those who profess to have "One Lord, one Faith, one Baptism," will recognise the consequent duty of joining their intercession to the Redeemer's dying prayer, "that they all may be one, as Thou, Father, art in Me, and I in Thee, that they also may be one in Us, that the world may believe that Thou hast sent Me." To all, then, who, while they lament the divisions among Christians, look forward for their healing mainly to a corporate reunion of those three great bodies which claim for themselves the inheritance of the priesthood and the name of Catholic, an appeal is made. They are not asked to compromise any principles which they rightly or wrongly hold dear. They are simply asked to unite for the promotion of a high and holy end, in reliance on the promise of our Divine Lord, "that whatsoever we shall ask in prayer, believing, we shall receive;" and that "if two or three agree on earth as touching anything that they shall ask, it shall be done for them of my Father who is in heaven." The daily use of a short form of prayer, together with one "Our

Father," for the intention of the Association, is the only obligation incurred by those who join it; to which is added, in the case of priests, the offering, at least once in three months, of the Holy Sacrifice, for the same intention.'

Certain Catholic names appeared in the list of its members, and its chief promoters were understood to assert that not a few Catholics were inscribed in its books. This is perhaps not far from accurate, inasmuch as it is known that the promoters of the scheme had manifested much activity in seeking the names of Catholics, especially on the continent; and that Catholics abroad are hardly on their guard against enterprises, not unfrequent among us, of which their own countries afford no example. Moreover, both abroad and in England the very name of unity is dear to every Catholic heart, and every one who utters it speaks the password to our goodwill. A Catholic, in proportion to his love to the Church of God, and of Jesus, Who in dying for us laid the law of unity upon us, will always mourn over the schisms which men have made, and be ready to give not his name only, but his life, if he could heal them. It is not wonderful, therefore, if some fervent minds should have consented to unite in this association. Others again were involved in it with more simplicity on their own part, and I fear, from their statements, less on that of those who invited them.

A Review setting forth the principles of the Association, and the opinion of individuals composing it, is published every two months. Certain Catholics were induced to unite in it; and statements purporting to come from Catholic hands have appeared in it, which compelled the Bishops of England to take cognizance of the Review and of the Association.

The matter was therefore referred by the united act of the Episcopate in England to the Holy Office, in the month of April 1864. The answer was dated on Sept. 16, 1864, and contains an enunciation of the following principles:

1. That the theory that Christendom or the Christian Church consists of three parts, the Roman, the Greek, and the Anglican, is a heresy overthrowing the nature of unity, and the Divine constitution of the Church. 'Fundamentum cui ipsa innititur hujusmodi est quod divinam Ecclesiæ constitutionem susque deque vertit. Tota enim in eo est ut supponat veram Jesu Christi Ecclesiam constare partim ex Romana Ecclesia per universum orbem diffusa et propagata, partim vero ex schismate Photiano et ex Anglicana hæresi, quibus æque ac Ecclesiæ Romanæ unus sit Dominus, una fides, et unum baptisma.'*

2. That to unite in an association of prayer with those who hold this theory is unlawful, inasmuch as it is an implicit adhesion to heresy, and to an intention stained with heresy. 'At quod Christi fideles et ecclesiastici viri hæreticorum ductu, et quod pejus est, juxta intentionem hæresi quam maxime pollutam

---

* S. R. I. Epist. ad omnes Angliæ Episcopos.

et infectam pro christiana unitate orent, tolerari nullo modo potest.'*

3. That such association favours indifferentism, and is therefore scandalous. 'Conspirantes in eam indifferentismo favent, et scandalum ingerunt.'†

The Holy Office therefore concludes by strictly prohibiting the faithful to inscribe themselves in it, or in any way whatsoever to show it favour. 'Maxima igitur sollicitudine curandum est ne Catholici, vel specie pietatis vel mala sententia decepti, societati de qua hic habitus est sermo aliisque similibus adscribantur, vel quoquomodo faveant.'

On the publication of this answer, the promoters of the Association addressed a letter to His Eminence Cardinal Patrizi, by whom, as Secretary of the Holy Office, the letter had been signed, saying that they had read it with great sorrow; that they had never affirmed that there are three Churches which with equal right (*æquo jure*) claim the name of Catholic; that they spoke only of *fact*, not of *right* (*facti, non juris*); that they never contemplated the reunion of three bodies holding discordant doctrines, but a reunion in truth; that the 'Union Review' had only a fortuitous connection with the Association, and conveyed only the opinions of individuals.

This address was signed by 198 Clergy of the Church of England.

The answer, dated Nov. 8, 1865, contains a lumi-

---

* S. R. I. Epist. ad omnes Angliæ Episcopos. † Ibid.

nous and precise enunciation of Catholic principles, of which I give a brief analysis, exhorting you to study the whole document, which is given in the Appendix, with the greatest exactness.

It affirms that all labour for unity is in vain, unless it be reduced to the principles upon which the Church was constituted by Christ in the beginning. Those principles it declares to be as follows:

1. That the unity of the Church is absolute and indivisible, and that the Church had never lost its unity, nor for so much as a moment of time ever can. 'Christi Ecclesia suam unitatem numquam amisit: numquam ne brevissimo quidem temporis intervallo amittet.' There is, therefore, both *de jure* and *de facto*, only one Church; one by a numerical and exclusive unity.

2. That the Church of Christ is indefectible, not only in duration, but in doctrine, or in other words, that it is infallible, which is a Divine endowment bestowed upon it by its Head; and that the infallibility of the Church is a dogma of the faith. 'Quod si Ecclesia Christi indefectibilis prorsus est, sponte sequitur eam infallibilem quoque dici et credi debere in Evangelica doctrina tradenda; quam infallibilitatis prærogativam Christum Dominum Ecclesiæ suæ, cujus Ipse est caput, sponsus, et lapis angularis, mirabili munere contulisse inconcussum est Catholicæ fidei dogma.'

* Second Letter of Holy Office addressed to Members of the Association, &c. &c.

3. That the Primacy of the Visible Head is of Divine institution, and was ordained to generate and to preserve the unity both of faith and of communion, that is, both internal and external, of which the See of Peter is both the centre and the bond. 'Jam non minus certum atque exploratum est Christum Jesum, ut fidei communionisque unitas in Ecclesia gigneretur ac perpetuo servaretur, utque capite constituto schismatis tolleretur occasio, Beatissimum Petrum præ cæteris Apostolis, tamquam illorum principem et ejusdem unitatis centrum et vinculum conspicuum, singulari providentia elegisse.'

4. That therefore the Catholic and Roman Church alone has received the name of Catholic. 'Ecclesia sancta, Ecclesia una, Ecclesia vera, Ecclesia Catholica, quæ Catholica nominatur non solum a suis, verum etiam ab omnibus inimicis, sicque ipsum Catholicæ nomen sola obtinuit.'

5. That no one can give to any other body the name of Catholic without incurring manifest heresy, 'citra manifestam hæresim.'

6. That whosoever is separated from the one and only Catholic Church, howsoever well he may believe himself to live, by this one sin of separation from the unity of Christ, is in the state of wrath. 'A qua quisque fuerit separatus, quantumlibet laudabiliter se vivere existimet, hoc solo scelere quod a Christi unitate disjunctus est, non habebit vitam, sed ira Dei manet super eum.'

7. That every several soul under pain of losing

eternal life is bound to enter the only Church of Christ, out of which is neither absolution nor entrance into the kingdom of heaven. 'Quicumque ab unitate fidei vel societate illius [Beati Petri] quolibet modo semetipsos segregant, tales nec vinculis peccatorum absolvi nec januam possint regni cœlestis ingredi.'

Such are the principles on which the Supreme Authority of the Holy Office exhorts the members of this Association to hasten from their disinherited separation into the inheritance of Christ. 'Ab exhæredata præcisione fugientes in hæreditatem Christi.'

Inasmuch, then, as these two letters of the Holy Office have been communicated to me both for my guidance and for yours, it is my duty to draw out the reasons which have called them forth, and the course which it is our duty to pursue towards those to whom these letters refer.

On the first principle of the former letter of the Holy Office, namely, 'that the theory that Christendom or the Christian Church consists of three parts, the Roman, the Greek, and the Anglican, is a heresy, overthrowing the nature of unity, and the Divine constitution of the Church,' we will for the present refrain from speaking, as it will fall more properly under the comments required hereafter by the second letter.

The second principle follows by necessity, 'that to unite in such an association with those who hold this theory, is unlawful, inasmuch as it is an implicit adhesion to heresy, and to an intention stained with heresy.'

I will therefore dwell upon the third, inasmuch as it makes practical application of the two former, namely, 'that such an association favours indifferentism, and is therefore scandalous.'

The sum of these three principles is briefly this, that the indivisible and exclusive unity of the Church is a dogma of faith, and that all association in prayer with those who deny it is unlawful. It is on this, then, that I purpose more fully to speak.

And in so doing I shall be compelled to treat not only of the matter of the declaration given above, but also of the principles and opinions put forward in the 'Union Review,' and in other works which are but repetitions of the same. They represent a school: and though in the letter to the Cardinal Secretary of the Holy Office certain members of the association affirm that it has only an accidental relation to the 'Union Review,' it is my duty to treat of both, as the errors are identical; and therefore, whether they be related or no, we are in conscience bound to deal with both. What I say, therefore, will apply to all works containing the same errors, by whomsoever written, whether he be of the association or not. As my object is first truth, and then unity, and as I know that both unity and truth are obscured by any breach of charity, I shall treat of errors, not of names, impersonally, and as they exist, not in any particular writer, but in themselves;

and I shall endeavour to treat them with as little severity as duty to truth admits.

That an association to promote the reunion of England with the Catholic and Roman Church should exist, and that nearly two hundred clergymen of the Church of England, describing themselves as 'Deans, Canons, Parish Priests, and other Priests' of the Church of England, should address the Cardinal Secretary of the Holy Office, expressing this desire, are facts new in our history since the separation of England from Catholic unity. We do not regard this as a merely intellectual or natural event. We gladly recognise in it an influence and an impulse of supernatural grace. It is a wonderful reaction from the days within living memory when fidelity to the Church of England was measured by repulsion from the Church of Rome. It is as wonderful an evidence of the flow in the tide which has carried the minds of men onward for these thirty years nearer and nearer to the frontiers of the Catholic faith. It is a movement against the wind and tide of English tradition and of English prejudice; a supernatural movement like the attraction which drew those who were once farthest from the kingdom of heaven to the side of our Lord. A change has visibly passed over England. Thirty years ago its attitude towards the Catholic Church was either intense hostility or stagnant ignorance. It is not so now. There is indeed still much hostility and much ignorance. But the hostility is more civilised, and the ignorance is breached on all sides. We do not, however, over-estimate the importance of the movement of which this association is the advanced column. It must never be forgotten that the Church of England represents only one-half of the English people, and that the Anglican school represents only a portion of the Church of England, and that the Anglo-Catholic movement represents only a section of the Anglican school, and that the Unionist movement represents only a fraction of that section. Two hundred clergymen are a small proportion upon some seventeen thousand; and supposing many to agree with them who did not sign the letter to Rome, and many more to wish well to them, the whole is hardly an appreciable quantity upon the Church of England, and an inappreciable quantity upon the English people. We say this to moderate the anticipations of inconsiderate hope, not to chill the warmth of our sympathy with those who are feeling their way to the truth. One soul, as S. Charles was wont to say, is diocese enough for a Bishop; and a mere remnant stretching out their hands towards unity have a right to all our care. At the same time we must not forget that our mission is not only to a section or to a fraction who may be approaching nearer to us, but to the whole mass of the English people. If the handful who have come so near have a claim upon our sympathy, much more have the millions who are as sheep without a shepherd, wandering to and fro in 'the dark and windy day.'

Moreover, we owe an especial duty to the class of the English people in which descends the mid-stream of traditional hostility to the Catholic Church—that is, the middle class of educated and industrious men, the heart of English national life, vigorous, quiet, intelligent, and benevolent, though darkened by inherited prejudices, and narrowed by anti-Catholic faults. To this class above all we have a mission of charity, that is, to preach the truth in patience, and to wait till they will listen. From circumstances of birth and education, from historical contacts, and approximations of opinion, from social and political neighbourhood, and from manifold bonds of kindred, the Anglican system is more nearly related to the Catholic Church than the Baptist, Independent, Wesleyan, and other Nonconformist bodies. And yet to the Catholic Church the millions who are in separation from the Established Church are an object of the profoundest sympathy and charity. They are souls for whom Christ died, robbed of their inheritance by the Anglican separation, from which they by legitimate process have separated in turn. Their state of privation is all the less culpable, as they have been born into a diminished inheritance of truth with a greater difficulty of rising to it again. They are, moreover, marked by a multitude of high qualities of zeal, devotion to duty, conscientious fidelity to what they believe. If they are rougher in their language against the Catholic Church, they are more generous and candid adversaries, more vehement but less bitter, and altogether free from the littleness of personality and petty faults which sometimes stain the controversy of those who are intellectually nearer to the truth. For such men it is our duty to cherish a warm charity and a true respect, and not disproportionately to waste upon those who stand nearer to us the time and the sympathy which is their due. The time is come that the Catholic Church should speak, face to face, calmly and uncontroversially to the millions of the English people who lie on the other side of the Anglican Establishment.

It may seem a strange and invidious thing for us who witness for the unity of the Church throughout the world to be tardy in going forth to meet those who approach us with invitations to union. This slowness is not, God knows, from indifference to division, or from disregard to the miseries and dangers of schism, or from insensibility to the dishonour of our Divine Master. For my own part, if I may speak of myself, it is more than a quarter of a century since the thought and name of unity so filled my whole mind that it has been often turned to my reproach. In all these years it has been my heart's desire and prayer, not only to see the members of the Anglican body gathered into Catholic unity, but the millions of Dissenters, that is, the whole English people, especially the multitude of its noble-hearted poor, united once more in the bond of peace and truth. We believe union to be a very precious gift, and only less precious than truth. There is nothing we would not do or suffer, by the grace of God, to effect or to promote the reunion of all, or of any who are out of the fold, to the unity of the Church. We heartily pray, therefore, that He who has inspired and nurtured this desire of union may mature and perfect it; that He will remove all that hinders its accomplishment, purifying the hearts of men from all attachment to their errors and their separations, and cleansing their intelligence to see the immutable faith and sole unity of the Catholic and Roman Church. On our part, all that can cherish and foster these yearnings shall be done. The vision of England Catholic once more, its true and energetic people once more elevated by faith to the higher instincts of the Catholic Church; our domestic schisms healed, our bitter controversies ended, and all our powers turned from mutual conflict, upon the subjugation of the sin and unbelief which, day and night, devours souls on every side: all this is as beautiful and fascinating as the image of the Heavenly Jerusalem which the Apostle saw coming down from heaven. There is only one thing more beautiful and more commanding, and that is the Heavenly Jerusalem itself, not in image, but in reality; the Holy Church throughout the world in all the perfect symmetry of unity and truth, indefectible and infallible, incorruptible and changeless, the mother of us all, the kingdom of God on earth.

We are ready to purchase the reunion of our separated brethren at any cost less than the sacrifice of a jot or a tittle of the supernatural order of unity and faith. When, some fifty years ago, a writer more zealous than circumspect spoke of a reunion of the Anglican and Catholic Churches, Bishop Milner, with his vigorous common sense and his high Catholic instinct, answered, 'If we should unite ourselves with it, the Universal Church would disunite itself from us.' This is the only price we cannot give for even so great a happiness as the reconciliation of England. Nor must we be misjudged for this. It is not that we will not, but that we cannot. We cannot barter, or give that which is not our own. The Divine and infallible authority of the Church sets the limits to our powers and our desires. We can offer unity only on the condition on which we hold it—unconditional submission to the living and perpetual voice of the Church of God. If this be refused, it is not we who hinder unity. For it is not we who impose this condition, but the Spirit of Truth who abides in the Church for ever.

Thus much we have said, lest we should seem to forget our mission to the great people of England, in our contact with the little band who are advancing with swords wreathed in myrtle. Nevertheless with them we are willing to deal with all charity, though from the right and centre of their array we still hear the cry of 'No peace with Rome.' We thank God that there are to be found ten men who desire to be restored to the centre of unity. We should have to answer to the Good Shepherd, if so much as one of His sheep were frayed away from the fold by harsh voices or rough handling on our part. Charity, in all its forms and instincts, of patience, tenderness, forbearance, hopefulness, and gentleness, is our duty as Pastors. But we owe them more than this. They have a right to the whole truth, and we are bound in duty to declare it to them. In this the beloved disciple is our pattern, the apostle of charity and of dogma, the most ardent in love to all men, the most inflexible for the doctrines of faith. It is startling to hear the disciple who lay upon the breast of Jesus say, 'If any man come to you and bring not this doctrine, receive him not into the house, nor say to him God speed you, for he that saith unto him God speed you, communicateth with his wicked works.' *

It would be contrary to charity to put a straw across the path of those who profess to desire union. But there is something more divine than union, that is, the Faith. It was to declare this law of His kingdom that our Divine Lord said, 'Do not think that I came to send peace upon earth; I came not to send peace, but the sword': † a Divine saying, most necessary in these days, when precision of doctrine is denounced as uncharitable, and dogma as the bar to union. It is this which the Holy Office has detected, with the true instinct of Rome, in the Association before us.

It is not lawful, then, for a Catholic to hold him-

---

* 2 S. John, 10, 11.   † S. Matth. x. 34.

self in a passive attitude towards any error contrary to faith. Therefore, it is not lawful for him to unite in prayer with those who hold such error. The fidelity he owes to the dogma of faith forbids it. 'Lex orandi,' as S. Augustine teaches, 'est lex credendi.' And this we shall see more clearly, by drawing out briefly what dogma is, and what are its obligations upon the conscience. It is the more necessary to do so, because it is precisely on this point that the Catholic Church is diametrically in conflict with the mind of the nineteenth century, and, so far as it utters itself in clamour, with the popular opinion of England. The Church is definite, precise, and peremptory in its declarations of doctrine. It refuses all compromise, transaction, or confusion of the terms and limits of its definitions. It is intolerant not only of contradiction, but of deviation. It excludes every formula but its own. The world is moving in the reverse direction. It is throwing everything open, levelling boundaries, taking in all forms of opinion, comprehending all sects of Christians, by eliminating all their differences, and finding a higher generality, a *summum genus* which embraces all. The Humanitarians merge all religion in Naturalism, the Unitarians in Christian morality, the Latitudinarians in the residuum of Christianity which survives the elimination of differences among Protestants, the Anglicans in an imaginary faith of the undivided Church, the Unionists in an agreement of the universal Church which shall neither be the

Thirty-nine Articles as they are understood by Englishmen, nor the Council of Trent as understood by Catholics, but the text of both, understood in a sense known neither to the Church of England nor to the Church of Rome; a doctrine wider than either, compared with which the faith and theology of the Church is denounced as narrow and sectarian. Such are the pretensions of a series and gradation of irreconcilable schools, conflicting with one another, agreed in nothing but common hostility to the only Church which is inflexible in dogma, and immutable in refusing all comprehension by way of compromise, and all contact with those who are without its unity. No wonder we are thought to be narrow, sectarian, and uncharitable. Nothing but a divine law could justify such a course. But such a law there is, which more than justifies. It binds the conscience of every member of the Church, from the Sovereign Pontiff to the little child in a Catholic school, to the divine unity of truth. For what is dogma but the true intellectual apprehension, and the true verbal expression of the truths and facts of the Divine Revelation? It is an eternal truth that there is one God in three Persons; the doctrine of Trinity in Unity is a dogma. It is a divine fact that the Son of God was made Man; the Incarnation is a dogma. It is a divine fact that the Holy Ghost came on the day of Pentecost, perfected and animated the Church with His presence, endowed it with an indivisible unity and a continuous infallibility, in virtue of His own perpetual presence and assistance; the conception and expression of all these divine operations is dogma. So I might enumerate all the doctrines of the faith. They are outlines traced upon the intelligence of the mystical body by the Spirit of God; the reflection of the mind of God in the mind of the Church, and the enunciation of the divine truths and facts so apprehended in words which truly and adequately express them. The perpetual knowledge and perpetual enunciation of these truths and facts, by the perpetual presence and assistance of the Holy Ghost, is the infallibility of the Church, or, in other words, the perpetuity of the Divine Revelation, in virtue of a divine guidance to the Church in all ages, in the nineteenth as in the first. How, then, can the Church cease to be dogmatic, without betraying its divine trust, and ceasing to witness for God?

It is also in behalf of the human reason itself, of its freedom and its perfection, that the Church is jealous in its custody of dogma. What axioms are to science, dogma is to theology. As there can be no science without fixed principles and primary certainties, so there can be no knowledge of God, nor of His revelation, without fixed and primary truths. Such are the doctrines of the faith delivered to us by the perpetual and divine office of the Church. The intellect of man is feeble and vacillating until it has certain scientific principles to start from. These once given, it acquires firmness and power of advance. One truth scientifically proved, becomes the basis of many.

The physical sciences, each in their kind, are proof of this. The same is true in the science of God. The truths of the natural order are confirmed and perfected by revelation. On the basis of natural truths rests, by the Divine disposition, the order of revealed truths, such as the Holy Trinity, the Incarnation, the Church and its supernatural endowments. The horizon of the human reason is therefore expanded by revelation, and the reason is elevated above its natural powers. And in this both its freedom and its perfection is secured. It is no bondage to know the truth, and no freedom to be in doubt. And yet they who know the truth are not free to contradict it; and they that are in doubt have the liberty of wandering out of the way. The law of gravitation once demonstrated, took away the liberty of contradicting it: and yet no man considers himself to be in bondage. All science limits the reason by the boundaries of its own certainty: but we do not therefore think men of science to be intellectual slaves. So is it with the science of God. We are limited by Divine Revelation, and by the infallibility of the Church, to believe in the Holy Trinity, the Incarnation, and the whole dogma of faith; but we are not therefore slaves, but freemen. We are redeemed from doubt and error, and from that which is both at once, from the guidance of the blind, the theology of human teachers, by the presence and office of a Divine. 'You shall know the truth, and the truth shall make you free.' And not free only, but perfect;

for the human reason advances to its perfection in proportion as it is conformed to the Divine. The dogma of faith is the mind of God, and theology is the science of God; and they that are most fully illuminated by it, are the most conformed to the Divine intelligence, which conformity is the perfection of the reason of man.

And once more, as the Holy Office affirms, there is no unity possible except by the way of truth. Truth first, unity afterwards; truth the cause, unity the effect. To invert this order is to overthrow the Divine procedure. The unity of Babel ended in confusion; the unity of Pentecost fused all nations in one body by the one dogma of faith. To unite the Anglican, the Greek, and the Catholic Church in any conceivable way could only end in a Babel of tongues, intellects, and wills. The intrinsic repulsions of the three are irresistible. Union is not unity. Heterogeneous and repugnant things may be arbitrarily tied together, but this is not unity. Union has in itself no assimilating power. Closer contact elicits the repugnances which rend all external bonds asunder. Truth alone generates unity. It was the dogma of faith which united the intellects of men as one intelligence The unity of truth generated its universality. The faith is Catholic, not only because it is spread throughout the world, but because throughout the world it is one and the same. The unity of the faith signifies that it is the same in every place. If it were not the same it would not be universal. Identity is the condition both of unity and of universality. From this springs the supernatural harmony of the human intelligence, spreading throughout the Church and reaching throughout all its ages. The dogma of faith has made it one by the assimilating power of the one science of God. From this unity of intellects has sprung the unity of wills. The unity of the Church is created by the submission of all wills to one Divine Teacher through the pastors of the Church, especially the one who is supreme on earth. Submission to one authority by an inevitable consequence draws after it unity of communion. One authority and one communion; 'One body, one spirit;' indivisible because intrinsically one; united both in intellect and will by the indivisible truth and charity of the Holy Ghost, by whom the Church is compacted, animated, and sustained. To countenance the assumption of the name of Catholic by any bodies in separation from, and in contradiction to, the one only Church, by so much as a silent or passive association, cannot be free from an implicit adhesion to heresy.

For this cause the Holy Office forbids the faithful to be united, or in any way whatsoever to show favour to an association which puts union before truth, contradicting thereby the Divine order of grace, and inverting the process by which the Church has been founded and perfected. They who seek truth before union are in the path in which the Son of God has always led His disciples to suffer for His sake. They who seek union before truth fall into heresy, or into indifference, and 'the rent is made worse.'

Once more: dogma is the way of salvation, and the Church is bound to its inflexible maintenance, not only by the obligation of truth, but also by the obligation of charity for the salvation of mankind. It is a dogma of faith that 'there is no other name under heaven given among men whereby we must be saved.' Salvation through the Name of Jesus is an absolute and exclusive condition.

Again: that there is 'one baptism for the remission of sins,' and that there is no salvation for those who reject it, is a dogma necessary to salvation, on which the Church could not falter without violating both truth and charity, and incurring the guilt of losing souls for whom Christ died.

In like manner, that there is 'one fold under one Shepherd,' and that the one fold is undivided and indivisible, is a dogma as divine and as inflexible as the unity of the Saving Name and of the necessity of baptism. We are as much bound, under pain of eternal death, to bear witness that without the Church is no salvation, as without baptism is no regeneration, and without the Name of Jesus no entrance into eternal life. In the old law it was written, 'Cursed be he that removeth his neighbour's landmark.'* And what is the visible unity of the Church

---

* Deut. xxvii. 17.

but the landmark which God has set up to bound the Fold of Salvation? They who deny its numerical and indivisible unity remove the landmark of God. They who teach that the Anglican separation and the Greek schism are parts of the Catholic Church violate a dogma of faith, destroy the boundaries of truth and falsehood, and 'cause the blind to go out of their way.'* The inflexible and exclusive dogmatic teaching of the Church, intolerant of all compromise and of all contact with error, is the voice of charity. As lighthouses are set up along dangerous coasts to guard seamen in the storms of night, so are the exclusive dogmas of the one Name, one Baptism, one Fold. To obscure these lights, much more to quench them, is cruelty to man. They who destroy sea-lights are enemies of the human race; much more they who cloud and confuse the distinctions which mark off the truths of God from the errors of men.

Lastly: not only charity to men but fidelity to God binds us to the most explicit and exclusive declaration of the truth, and the most vigilant refusal to unite even passively in any association with error. For truth is the Word of God; our Divine Lord identifies it with Himself and Himself with it. He says, 'I am .. the Truth.'† The truth is, therefore, not a theory, but a Person, and we owe to it a personal fidelity. Every particle of His word, and every precept of His will, is a personal obligation on our con-

---

* Deut. xxvii. 18. † S. John, xiv. 6.

science. The exclusive unity of His Church is both a Divine truth and a Divine precept, from which we cannot swerve without personal infidelity to Him.

Moreover, dogma is the mind of the Spirit of Truth, Who inhabits the only Church of God, and makes it the organ of His voice. To unite in prayer with those who deny the unity of His temple and the organ of His voice, who affirm that He is silent, and that because of schism He cannot speak, or, worse than all, that He speaks through three *de facto* Churches in perpetual contradiction and in perpetual conflict, is an infidelity to the Person of the Spirit of Truth, and a dishonour to His presence and His office.

Lastly, it is an infidelity to the Father of Lights, who has so revealed His mind and His will as to make His Church the light of the world, that is, the self-evident witness, more manifest than all reasonings, more luminous than all proofs, as 'a city seated on a mountain,' visible to all whose eyes are open.

The first theological virtue infused into us in our baptism—the grace of faith, and the union of our hearts to the Divine truth delivered by the Church—forbids even a passive union with those who violate an article of the Baptismal Creed, and obscure the way of salvation.

The Holy Office has declared with a dignified calmness of language, that for 'the disciples of Christ and the ministers of His Church to pray for the unity of Christendom, at the invitation of those who are in heresy, and in union with an intention eminently depraved and infected by heresy, can in no way be tolerated.' We may pray for them, but not with them; and all the more pray for them as we are bound to bear active and explicit witness against all heresy, material or formal, as it may be, and the peril in which its teachers stand, by refusing all communion with them even in prayer. The only spiritual association founded by God is the Church of God.

Such, then, is the substance of the first letter.

We may now proceed to the second.

The adherents of the Association complained, as I have said, in their letter to his Eminence Cardinal Patrizi, that they had been misunderstood; that they did not affirm the existence of three Churches or of three parts of the Church 'æquo jure,' but only 'de facto;' that they did not desire reunion with a permanence of conflicting doctrines, from which, they admitted, that discord, under the same roof, rather than ecclesiastical unity, would arise.

To this the Holy Office answered, that there is but one principle of unity which is before all and generates all union, namely, Truth, working through the one and only Church united to its centre and bond of unity, the See of Peter. It affirmed also that to pray for the reunion of the Church, is to assume that it can be divided; that such an assumption is contrary to faith; that the unity of the Church never has been lost, nor ever can be; and that as its unity is perpetual, so is its infallibility, in the nineteenth century as in the first.

Now it is not my intention to enter into these propositions in detail. For you, Reverend and dear Brethren, it is needless. They are the principles of your whole life, the instinctive laws of your minds. For others I cannot now attempt an adequate treatment: and can only refer to what I have endeavoured to say as to the doctrine of the Church on the Temporal Mission of the Holy Ghost. But it is possible within our present limits and at this time to apply the principles of the Holy Office to the particular form of error which this Union movement has cast up. We may state it as follows:—The Church of Christ is one in origin, succession, and organisation; but not necessarily in communion. For six centuries or more it was united, till the East separated from the West: since then, it has indeed lost its perfection, but both parts continue to be the Church. While united it was infallible, and the faith received universally was certainly divine. After its division it continued to be infallible in all that was infallible before; but in all questions emerging after the division, it had no infallible voice or judgment to decide: neither could any decision be tested by the reception of the whole Church: the later divisions of the Reformation only reproduce the same anomalies in the West; the Anglican Church stands upon the same basis as the Greek; both contain the infallible truth of the undivided Church of the beginning; neither claims to be infallible in questions emerging now : the Church of England has not erred in its thirty-nine Articles ; and the Roman Church has not erred in its decrees at Trent; both are capable of a true interpretation, and both need a more perfect interpretation than either have as yet received. Such interpretation in the future is the basis of reunion, and the hope of Christendom; such was the position of Bossuet, and such they claim as their own; but the great hindrance to reunion is the perpetual expansion of Roman opinions, and their transformation into new articles of faith, as for instance, the Immaculate Conception, and the Ultramontane theories which make the Pope personally infallible, and the temporal power a dogma of faith.

Let us draw out what these propositions contain.

1. First, they deny the indivisible unity and perpetual infallibility of the Church, which are affirmed by the Holy Office in precise terms. This was not the position of Bossuet, who lays down as follows :—

'In the year 1542, when the Lutheran pestilence began to make havoc in this most Christian kingdom, the Doctors of Paris, assembled in Faculty, published these Articles:—

'Every Christian is bound firmly to believe that the Universal Church is One, visible on earth, which in faith and morals cannot err, and which all the faithful, in whatsoever pertains to faith and morals, are bound to obey.'

'It is certain that a General Council legitimately gathered together, representing the Universal Church, cannot err in its decisions in faith and morals.'

'Nor is it less certain that in the Church Militant there is, by Divine right, one Roman Pontiff, whom all Christians are bound to obey. This rule of faith, delivered by all the Gallican Bishops and Churches, received also by Royal authority and the consent of all Orders, has been published and preserved by the same.'*

2. Next, they deny the infallibility of the Council of Trent, of which Bossuet thus writes to Leibnitz:—

'To give a clear and final resolution of the doubts which are raised about the Council of Trent, certain principles must be presupposed:—

'1. That the infallibility which Jesus Christ has promised to His Church resides in the whole body.

'2. That this infallibility, inasmuch as it consists, not in receiving, but in teaching the truth, resides in the order of Pastors, who succeed the Apostles, to whom the promise of Jesus Christ was made.

'3. That Bishops or Pastors, who are not ordained by and in this succession, have no part in the promise.

'4. That the Bishops or principal Pastors, who have been ordained in that succession, if they renounce the faith of their consecrators, that is to say, the faith which is in vigour in the whole body of the Episcopate and of the Church, would renounce at the same time their part in the promise, because they renounce the succession, the continuity, and perpetuity of the doctrine.

'5. That the Bishops and principal Pastors instituted in virtue of the promise, and abiding in the faith and the communion of the body where they have been consecrated, are able to bear witness to their faith, either by their unanimous preaching throughout the Catholic Church dispersed, or by an express judgment made in a legitimate Council. In either way their authority is equally infallible, and their doctrine equally certain. In the former way, because it is

---

* Defens. Declarat. Cleri Gallicani, ed. Luxemb. 1730, tom. i. p. 3.

to that body thus outwardly dispersed, but united by the Holy Ghost, that the infallibility of the Church is attached; in the latter, because that body, being infallible, the Assembly which truly represents it, that is to say, the Council, has the same privilege, and can say, after the manner of the Apostles, "It seemed good to the Holy Ghost and to us."

'6. He adds that such a Council truly represents the Catholic Church, if its decrees be received by it.'

Bossuet sums up with this judicial sentence:—

'Those who will not accept these principles must never hope for any union with us, because they would never accept, but in words, the infallibility of the Church, which is the only solid principle of the reunion of Christians.

'On these principles it is easy to resolve all the doubts concerning the Council of Trent in that which regards the faith, as it is certain that it is received and approved in that respect by the whole body of the Churches which are united in communion with that of Rome, which alone we recognise as Catholic, which Churches would no more reject its authority than they would that of the Council of Nice.'*

3. Lastly, they deny the Council of Trent to be œcumenical, which Bossuet recognised as of equal authority with the Council of Nice. His words seem to be written for the present day, and for this peculiar phase of anti-Catholic thought.

In his project for the reunion between the Catholics and Protestants of Germany, he says: 'As to the objection of the Protestants that the Council of Trent was not œcumenical, because they did not sit·

---

* Projet de Réunion entre les Catholiques et les Protestants d'Allemagne. Lettre XXII.

in it as judges, together with the Catholic Bishops, but sentence was passed by the adverse party; if their complaints were admitted there could never have been any Council, nor ever can be, inasmuch as neither did the Council of Nice admit as judges the Novatians and Donatists, or others already in any way separate from the Church; nor can heretics be ever judged, except by Catholics; nor they who secede from the Church, except by those who maintain its unity. Neither did the Lutherans, when in their synods they condemned the Zwinglians, have them as assessors; nor did justice permit that the Catholic Church should be judged by the English, Danish, Swedish Bishops, who professed open enmity against it, and had seceded from the Roman Church as impious, idolatrous and antichristian.'

The sum of Bossuet's judgment is given in these words:—' Nothing, therefore, will ever be done either by the Roman Pontiff, or by any Catholic whatsoever, by which the Tridentine Decrees of Faith can be shaken.'*

To what end, then, do men appeal to Bossuet, if they do not believe with Bossuet? Is it for the purpose of opposing the infallibility of the Pope? But that will not evade the infallibility of the Church. If Bossuet thought that the infallibility of the Pope *ex cathedrâ* could in his day be denied *salva fidei compage*,

---

* Bossuet, Projet de Réunion entre les Catholiques et les Protestants d'Allemagne, par. iii. art. 2. Œuvres de Bossuet, tom. viii. p. 637.. Paris, 1846.

most assuredly he taught that no man could deny the infallibility of the Church without explicit heresy. If he taught that the reception of definitions by the Church was the test of their infallible certainty, he believed that Church to be the sole Catholic and Roman Church, in union with the See of Peter and exclusive of the Greek and Anglican schisms. What do they gain who appeal to Bossuet, but a greater condemnation? Out of their own mouth comes the sentence. Not only those who hold the infallibility of the Roman Pontiff condemn them, but all those who hold only the infallibility of the Church. Gallicanism, the minimum of Catholic truth, condemns them as peremptorily as the highest Ultramontane theology. It is dangerous to use arguments *ad invidiam*, and for those who are without to appeal to any tribunal within the Catholic unity. We may say to them as S. Augustine said to the Donatists who quoted the example of S. Cyprian against him: 'You object to us the letters of Cyprian, the judgment of Cyprian, the council of Cyprian; why put forward the authority of Cyprian for your schism, and reject his example which witnesses for the unity of the Church?' *
We see Bossuet in Catholic unity; we see you in separation. Place yourselves where Bossuet lived and died, and then quote Bossuet. Being where you are, his name is a sentence against you.

The denial of the perpetual Divine assistance by

---

* S. Aug. de Baptismo contra Donatistas, lib. ii. sec. 4.

which the Church is preserved from error, has led some to say that they accept the decrees of the Council of Trent, but not the interpretation of them. The Church of England is supposed to be found, not in the multitudinous contradictions of its living teachers, but only in the passive letter of its formularies. The Church of Rome is supposed not to be found in its dogmatic decrees, but in any obscure writer whose books may not be censured. Still, even here truth is justified. The Church is to be found in its living voice; and its living voice is the true, and only true, and only authoritative interpretation of its formularies. By a law of natural production the formularies of the Church of England have generated contradictions over its whole surface; by a law of supernatural progression the decrees of Trent have expanded into a wide-spread and exuberant theology, dogmatic and mystical, pervading both the head and the heart, reaching far beyond the letter, as the spread of a cedar reaches on all sides beyond its centre, but is firmly and intrinsically united to its root, from which it derives life, symmetry, and substance.

When we call this living mind of the Church the true interpretation of the dogma of the faith, we need not remind you, Reverend Brethren, that in the Bull of Pius IV., confirmed and published by the Holy Council of Trent, the Sovereign Pontiff explicitly reserved to himself the interpretation of its decrees as follows:—

'And further, to avoid perversion and confusion which might arise if it were permitted to every one according to his will to put forth his commentaries and interpretations of the decrees of the Council, we inhibit by apostolical authority to all persons of whatsoever order, condition or degree, whether ecclesiastical or lay, with whatsoever power they may be invested, if they be prelates, under the pain of interdict of entering the Church, and others, whosoever they be, under pain of excommunication *latæ sententiæ*, that no one, without our authority, venture to put forth any commentaries, glosses, annotations, *scholia*, or any kind of interpretation on the decrees of the same Synod, or to determine anything under whatsoever title, even under pretext of a greater confirmation or furtherance of the decrees, or any pretended reason. But if any one shall find in the same decrees any obscurity of language or of law, and for that cause any interpretation or decision shall seem to be needed, let him ascend into the place which the Lord hath chosen, that is, to the Apostolic See, the Guide of all the Faithful, whose authority the Holy Synod itself so reverently acknowledged. We therefore reserve to ourselves, according as the Holy Synod itself enjoined, the declaration and decision of all questions which may arise from its decrees.'*

* Bulla *Benedictus Deus* Pii IV. sup confirm. Conc. Trid. : 'Ad vitandum præterea perversionem et confusionem, quæ oriri posset, si unicuique liceret, prout ei liberet, in decreta concilii commentarios et interpretationes suas edere, apostolica auctoritate inhibemus omnibus, tam ecclesiasticis personis, cujuscumque sint ordinis, conditionis, et gradus, quam laicis, quocunque honore ac potestate præditis, prælatis quidem sub interdicti ingressus ecclesiæ, aliis vero quicumque, fuerint sub excommunicationis latæ sententiæ pœnis, ne quis sine auctoritate nostra audeat ullos commentarios, glossas, annotationes, scholia, ullumve omnino interpretationis genus super ipsius concilii decretis quocunque modo edere, aut quicquam quocunque nomine, etiam sub prætextu majoris decretorum corroborationis aut executionis, aliove quæsito colore statuere. Si cui vero in eis aliquid obscurius dictum et statutum fuisse, eamque ob causam

We have, therefore, a body of principles which govern the interpretation of dogmatic definitions, and regulate the living teaching of the Church.

1. All interpretations emanating from Pontifical authority are certainly infallible.

2. All decisions and doctrines taught by inferior tribunals or by theological schools, so long as they are not condemned by the Church, being publicly known and held in the presence of the supreme authority, may be presumed to be free from all error against faith or morals.

Of the first class are the copious and luminous decisions of the Pontiffs, S. Pius V., Innocent X., and Alexander VII., in the doctrines of grace contained in the condemned propositions of Baius and Jansenius, and the like.

Of the second class are all theological and devotional works which the Church has not censured. If they be publicly known and tolerated they may be presumed to be conformable to the dogma of faith, and to be innocent. They might not, perhaps, deserve it. They might enjoy rather impunity than toleration. Yet, till noted with censure they are in possession; like as, by our common law, a man is

---

interpretatione aut decisione aliqua egere visum fuerit, ascendat ad locum quem Deus elegit, ad sedem videlicet apostolicam, omnium fidelium magistram, cujus auctoritatem etiam ipsa sancta synodus tam reverenter agnovit. Nos enim difficultates et controversias, si quæ ex eis decretis ortæ fuerint, nobis declarandas et decidendas, quemadmodum ipsa quoque sancta synodus decrevit, reservamus.'

innocent till he is found guilty. It is, indeed, a part of fidelity to truth, and of charity to souls, not to give impunity to errors in theology or devotion; and the Catholic instincts of pastors and people are quick and vigilant to detect any unsoundness, and to bring it under judicial examination. No great error passes undiscovered. And this is a presumption that whatsoever is publicly known and tolerated, whatever may be thought of it, cannot be contrary to faith or morals. But this does not make such teaching authoritative.

Nevertheless, we have no hesitation in saying, that whosoever shall rise up to condemn as pernicious what the public authority of the Church tolerates as innocent, is thereby guilty of temerity, and of immodesty. In so doing he would be ascribing to himself the supreme discernment which belongs to the Church alone. ' The spiritual man judgeth all things, and he himself is judged by no man.'* It would be the illuminism of the individual revising the discernment of the Church; the climax and efflorescence of the private judgment which criticises all things—first Scripture, then Fathers, then Churches, then Councils, then Pontiffs, finally the accumulated living Christianity of the Catholic Church, in which the heart and mind of Fathers, Councils, and Pontiffs breathe, and teach, and worship.

It would be, then, a want both of prudence and of charity to encourage those who indulge this habit of

* 1 Cor. ii. 15.

mind in looking for concessions and explanations, to make tolerable to them the decrees of the Catholic Church. Such a course simply indulges and confirms the habit of private judgment, brings those who practise and those who indulge it under the censure of several Pontiffs, and obscures the only true principle of divine faith.

To profess a readiness to accept the Council of Trent, if it be interpreted according to our own opinion, is not to subject ourselves to the authority of the Council, but to subject it to our own judgment. To say we will accept it as the basis of reunion if it mean so and so, is to say we will not accept it if it mean otherwise: or, again, if the Pope would declare that the Council of Trent never meant what we object to, we would receive it. But what if it should mean otherwise? To ask for an authoritative interpretation, without engaging to submit to it, is to play fast and loose. If the authoritative interpretation agree with our own, well and good. But what if it differs? In this way we should not receive it because of its authority, but because of its agreement with our private judgment. If it differ, it would not be authoritative to us. Is it possible that men of any clearness or coherence of mind can fail to see through the obscurity and inconsequence of this procedure? In what does it differ from the private judgment of the common and consistent Protestant, who judges for himself of the meaning of Scripture, except only in this, that he confines himself to one book, and they claim to judge of all the Fathers, Theologians, Councils, Pontiffs, and the whole Church in every age? The common Protestant passes dry-shod over all these without asking whether he agrees with them or not: the Anglo-Catholic summons and convenes them all before him; professes to recognise them for what they are, Fathers, Theologians, Councils, Pontiffs; acknowledges their special illumination, commission, and authority; but after all analyses, criticises, accepts, rejects their writings and their teaching with a final sentence that is an absolute superiority of judgment. In their opinion the Council of Trent is tolerable if it mean only what they mean; intolerable if it mean anything else: tolerable if it agree with Tract XC.; intolerable if it be in harmony with the faith, piety, devotion, and public worship of the Catholic and Roman Church throughout the world. Can private judgment exalt and enlarge itself beyond this girth and stature? Is there anything left on earth to be judged of; anything yet to pass under its analysis and its sentence; any tribunal standing, before which it is silent, or to which it inclines? It seems strange that good men do not perceive the moral fault of such pretensions, and men of intellect their incoherence. To read the pages of Holy Writ, luminous and simple as in great part they are, and, knowing no other teacher, neither Church nor Council, to walk humbly by the light of a few divine truths, reverently adoring many incomprehensible mysteries—this is intelligible, coherent, and comparatively modest. But to profess to believe in Saints, Doctors, and Councils, which, if they may err, still have a special guidance, and in the Church of God, inhabited by the Spirit of God, infallible for six hundred years, assisted still in its decrees, superior to all individual minds, the chief authority on earth, divinely ordained to guide men; and yet after this to criticise all its acts and utterances, from the Canons of Nice to the Decrees of Trent, from the Canon of Scripture declared by Pope Gelasius, to the Immaculate Conception declared by Pope Pius IX., and to propose this as the basis of reunion in the midst of the confusions of Anglicanism, is a process which I must refrain from characterising as it would demand. We should offend against both truth and charity if we were not to show with all fidelity and at all costs the impossibility of reunion on such terms. To receive the whole Council of Trent upon the principle of private judgment would make no man a Catholic. To receive the Council of Trent only because we critically believe its decrees to be true, and not because its decrees are infallible, is private judgment. We should not be submitting to them, but approving them. The formal motive of our approval would be not the divine authority of the Council, but the judgment of our private spirit. God forbid, Reverend and dear Brethren, that minds be so brought within the unity of the Church. It would multiply our number, but not multiply the faithful. It would be to introduce among us a new and un-Catholic element, a show of material agreement disguising a formal and vital contrariety. Much as we desire to gather souls into the only Ark of Salvation, we dare not do so at the sacrifice of truth. The admission of those who deny the infallibility of the living Church Catholic and Roman of this hour, would not be salvation to them. They would be as S. Augustine said, 'intus corpore, corde foris.' All encouragement to such habits of mind can only end in disappointment, and miseries worse than disappointment. It could only end in apostacies, and complaints not unjust that they had been deceived. They would 'go out from us because they are not of us.' It is far more truthful and charitable to say, firmly and plainly: The Church of God admits of no transactions. Recognition of its divine office, acknowledgment of previous error, submission to its divine voice—these and no others are the conditions of reunion.

Trusting to the unpopularity of what is called Ultramontanism, and to the popularity of all that encourages Nationalism, efforts have been studiously made for some years, and by writers of all kinds, sometimes, I grieve to say, by those who bore the name of Catholic, to represent as extreme, exclusive, and Ultramontane, all who believe the Holy See to be the Supreme Fountain of Faith and jurisdiction. This has been lately renewed under the form of seeking reunion on a Gallican basis, rejecting Ultramontane excesses, and appealing to the higher authority of the universal Church, to be ascertained hereafter by some process neither stated nor conceivable. You will not need, Reverend and dear Brethren, that I should point out to you that to refuse the Divine authority of the Church, speaking by its visible head, and to appeal from that authority even to a Council in the future, falls under the sentence of excommunication reserved to the Pope.

On a point of such gravity I think it well to give the summary of the Pontifical law. The appeal from the Pope to a future General Council is described by canonists as the crime of sacrilege against the primacy of the Sovereign Pontiff. Pius II. excommunicates all who so offend, and reserves their absolution to the Pope, declaring further that all who knowingly give counsel, help, or favour to those who so offend, incur the same pains and censures as the abettors of high treason and of heretical pravity.

And Julius II. declared that the same were to be held as true and undoubted schismatics, and of unsound opinions concerning the Catholic faith. Moreover, he extended all the above-named pains and censures to those who, by resolution, counsel, or deliberation, have either approved the words of others, or have given their opinion that an appeal from the Pope to a future General Council may, can, or ought to be made.*

* Thesaurus: De Pœnis Ecclesiasticis, ed. Giraldi, Romæ, 1831, p. 95:—
CAPUT I.
Appellantes a summo Pontifice ad futurum Concilium Generale.
Hoc est crimen sacrilegii contra primatum Pontificis Romani,

And further, it must be always borne in mind, and explicitly declared to our flocks, that the infallibility of the Pope, speaking *ex cathedrâ*, is an opinion protected by the highest authority. Alexander VIII., by a decree of December 7, 1690, that is, eight years after the Gallican declaration of 1682, condemned the following proposition: 'The assertion of the authority of the Roman Pontiff over General Councils, and his infallibility in determining questions of faith, is futile and

Cajet. &c. Est autem jure declaratum non licere appellare a sententia Romani Pontificis, *cap.* Nemo, *cap.* Aliorum facta, *cap.* Ipsi sunt, *cap.* Cuncta per mundum, &c. . . . Præterea in dicta Bulla Pii II. incipit *Execrabilis*, statutum est, ut appellantes a Papa ad futurum Concilium, vel scienter consilium, auxilium, aut favorem ad id praestantes, eas pœnas, et censuras incurrant, quas rei læsæ majestatis, et hæreticæ pravitatis fautores incurrere dignoscuntur.

Et Julius II. dicta Bulla, incipit *Suscepti*, § 5, confirmavit dictam Constitutionem Pii II. supplendo omnem defectum solemnitatis, etiam publicationis forte omissæ; et, § 6, declaravit dictos contravenientes non solum ipso facto incurrere in pœnas in dicta Bulla *Execrabilis* impositas, sed ipsos pro veris et indubitatis schismaticis, et de catholica fide male sentientibus habendos, pœnisque canonicis et legalibus contra tales impositis subjacere. Item omnes supradictas pœnas et censuras extendit ad eos qui decreverint, consuluerint, deliberaverint, aut aliorum dicta approbaverint, aut vocem dederint, ut ad futurum Concilium universale a Papa appellare liceat, possit vel debeat.

· Et merito quidem haec statuta sunt: nam appellans a Papa ad Concilium, in crimen rebellionis incurrit, quatenus sic appellando se subtrahit ab obedientia supremi sui Principis in damnum ejusdem Principis, ejusque supremi dominii, illud ad alium procurando convertere . . . Similiter quod tales sint schismatici, et de fide male sentientes, ait *Sylvest.*, &c. et alii communiter. . . . Et quod asserens licitum esse appellare a Papa ad futurum Concilium sint hæretici formaliter, tenet *S. Antonin.*, &c. . . . Unde sequitur tales incurrere in censuras et pœnas latas contra hæreticos.

has been often refuted.' The lightest censure inflicted by the decree on this proposition is that of temerity, and whosoever shall in public or in private maintain it, incurs excommunication reserved to the Pope. I say the lightest, because inasmuch as Theologians, such as Suarez and Bellarmine, hold the contrary of this proposition to be proximate to faith, it may be maintained with much reason that it is scandalous, savouring of heresy and proximate to heresy, and it is certain that to maintain it or to believe it, is a sin.*

But once more: we have said that this procedure obscures the principle of divine faith, which is the veracity of God proposing His revelations to us through the medium of His Church. It is no question at this day how God proposed His truth to man before His Church was instituted through the incarnation of His Son, nor how He may propose it now among those to whom His Church is not present. The question is for England at this day. The Catholic Church is present among us, visible and audible, proposing the whole revelation of God by the divine voice of His Holy Spirit. To criticise the decrees of Trent, before they believe or disbelieve their divine veracity, is evasion. To put forward lamentations over the onward course of the Church by accusing it of turning private opinions into dogmas of faith, is to beg the question. To accuse the Church of making new truths, is like

---

* Viva, Damnatæ Theses. Patavii, 1737, p. 495.

accusing it of worshipping a wafer. A Catholic major premiss and a Protestant minor makes a poor syllogism. To complain of Ultramontanism as the great obstacle to reunion, is to hide the true issue of the controversy. If the Pope be not infallible, at least the Church is. Let men submit to the infallibility of the Church, and we may then hear what they will say of the infallibility of the Pope. It is not Ultramontanism that demands their submission, but even Gallicanism. And it is Gallicanism that bars their way, until they have submitted with heart and head in faith both to the exclusive and indivisible unity, and the exclusive and perpetual infallibility of the Catholic and Roman Church.

Divine faith consists in an infusion of supernatural grace illuminating the intelligence to know and the heart to believe all that God has revealed and proposed to be believed. The proposition of the Church is the test of the Revelation of God. The Church proposes all that God has revealed, and nothing that He has not revealed. We have no contact with the Revelation of God, except through the proposition of the Church. We are in contact with the Scriptures, because the Church proposes them to us as the written word of God; we are in contact with tradition, because the Church proposes tradition to us as the unwritten word of God. We are in contact with antiquity, because the Church proposes antiquity as its own past experience. Antiquity is no more than a period in the mind of the Church: for the mind of the Church is continuous. It proposes to us now what it proposed in antiquity. Every age has its truths, terms, definitions; and all are guarded and laid up in the divine custody of the Church, and are proposed in every age as the householder ' bringeth forth things old and new:' the old new, because ever fresh; the new old, because they were from the beginning; though new errors demand new terms, and old truths need new fences to exclude new perversions. As Vincent of Lerins said, ' Non nova sed novè.'

The principle, or rule of divine faith, then, is this, that the enunciation of the Church of this hour is the test and evidence of the original Revelation. By this God speaks to our reason and our faith. To refuse this, is to reject the voice of God in the world. We have, in that case, no choice but to turn to human teachers and to human criticism.

It is strange that men of consecutive minds, who seem to have mastered the principle that the Church alone possesses the key of Scripture, and that the true mind of Scripture is to be known only as it is interpreted by the living mind of the Church, should not see that, à fortiori, by the same law, the sense of antiquity is to be known from the Church alone. It is in vain to answer to the Catholic: But we have antiquity before us, Fathers and Councils, facts and doctrines. The Protestant says the same to them in turn: We have Scripture before us, the Evangelists and the Apostles, the very words and deeds of our Divine Lord. The Protestant is comparatively consistent in rejecting the Church, and interpreting both Scripture and antiquity for himself. How is it coherent to interpret Scripture by the Church, and antiquity by private judgment; to affirm the Church to be the interpreter of Scripture, but not of antiquity—that is, of the written word of God, but not of its own words and acts, its own experience, and its own intentions? This is surely a confusion into which nothing but the stress of controversy could have driven cultivated and thoughtful men. Was it that the one theory was necessary against Dissenters, the other against Catholics?

The ultimate cause, indeed, probably is, that such reasoners have no adequate perception of the unity and continuity of the mind of the Church; and that, because they have no adequate perception of the perpetual presence and office of the Spirit of Truth in the Church. This one truth once fully seen, solves all, not only by way of authority, but by way of intelligent explanation. The Fathers were but the disciples of the Church, 'Doctores fidelium ecclesiæ discipuli.' What they taught they first learned; and the Church who taught them, both recognises her own teaching in their writings, even when the language may be less exact, and can correct it where it is equivocal, obscure, or erroneous.

The same is true of Councils, which are its own assemblies, and express its collective mind, with the sanction of its public authority. The Church of to-day sees its own mind, faith and morals, doctrine and discipline, not only in the first four Councils appealed to by Anglicans, but in the seven held to be general by the Greeks, and in the eleven which have continuously legislated and decreed, from the Second Council of Nice down to the Council of Trent. As the British empire knows the mind of its own legislature from its earliest parliaments to this day, and permits no man, be he subject, or prince, to contravene its authoritative interpretations, so, even in the natural order, the Catholic Church knows its own ancient statutes, and the acts of its own senate.

But more than this, the lineal and living consciousness of the Church has a higher fountain than the natural order. The perpetual knowledge and certainty of the revelation committed to its custody comes by a Divine assistance, as the revelation itself came by a Divine gift. The perpetuity of its infallibility is the permanence of the original revelation, by the perpetual presence of the same Divine Person from whom it flowed. Its onward progression in the explicit definition of truth is a property and an evidence of its perpetual divine office. When we enunciate these axioms of Catholic faith, we are accused of putting assertions for proofs. But it is the office of a divine teacher to assert and not to argue. The assertions of men are indeed no argument, but the assertion of the Church is proof in itself.

The denial of the perpetual Divine assistance of the Church has its newest form in the assertion that though the assistance be perpetual, yet we do not know when its exercise is to be expected. This comes strangely from those who say that the Church is divided, and that its divisions make the exercise of its infallible office at present impossible. They appear to admit that the assistance of the Holy Spirit is perpetual, but yet they affirm that it is not always. They appear to hold an intermittent operation of the Spirit of Truth, which gives no tests whereby it is to be discerned from the operation of human authority and of human teachers. The definition of the Immaculate Conception is accused as novel, unseasonable, and a hindrance to the reunion of Christendom. If true, why was it not defined before? If not necessary, why defined now?

To this we answer: When the disciples asked of our Divine Lord, 'Wilt thou at this time restore the kingdom to Israel?' He said, 'It is not for you to know the times or moments which the Father hath put in His own power. But you shall receive the power of the Holy Ghost coming upon you.'*
In these words He declared the sovereignty and secrecy of His government over the Church. He reserved to Himself the time and the season of His operations; but when they came, all men recognised in them His presence and His action. During the ten days between the Ascension and the day of Pen-

* Acts i. 7, 8.

tecost, they were in uncertainty as to the future, and what His words might mean. When the Holy Ghost descended all was manifest. No man could doubt that it was the operation of His will. So it may be said of the course and action of the Church. In the succession of its history from the declaration of the Consubstantiality of the Son to the Immaculate Conception of His Blessed Mother, there has been a line of definitions reaching through fifteen centuries of time. They who ask why the Immaculate Conception has been defined in the nineteenth century, would have asked why the 'homoousion' was defined in the fourth, or the two Natures in one Person in the fifth. To those who deny the perpetual Divine office of the Church, all this may indeed cause perplexity; but the perplexity arises not from the exercise of its Divine office by the Church, but from their denial of it. They are the makers of their own difficulties. To those who believe that the words of Jesus are verified to the letter, and that the Spirit of Truth perpetually abides with us in all the fulness of His operations, it is as obvious and as certain that the Church should infallibly declare the doctrines of the faith in the nineteenth as in the sixth or the fourth century. Nay, more; we believe that the discernment not only of the truth, but of the opportunity of declaring it, are both contained in the Divine assistance which guides the Church. We are sure that the 'homoousion' is true, and that the fourth century was the opportunity divinely chosen for its declaration. We know with the certainty of faith that the Immaculate Conception is true, and we are certain that this time was the opportunity divinely chosen for its definition. The event is proof. The times and the moments were uncertain before the event; after it they form a part of the Divine operation, and are declared by the fact. It is remarkable that the two questions proposed by the Sovereign Pontiff to the Bishops throughout the world were, not whether the doctrine of the Immaculate Conception were true; but first, whether it were definable, and second, if so, whether the time for defining it were come. Is it from want of knowledge, or accuracy of mind, that some have represented the Bishops of the Catholic world as divided about the truth of the Immaculate Conception? They all alike and with one voice proclaimed, and, as we are told even by an adversary, ostentatiously proclaimed, their belief of it. Some of them indeed doubted before the event, whether the time and the moment were come for the definition. And this has been used to create a rhetorical impression, on the minds of those who do not know the facts of the case, that they were opposed to the doctrine to be defined. The unreserved freedom with which a small number of the Bishops expressed their opinion, either that the doctrine was not capable of definition, or that the time for defining it was not opportune, made all the more striking their unanimity in believing it to be true, and the unhesitating firmness with which the Sovereign Pontiff proceeded to define it. A hostile critic has acutely remarked that the Pope knew the mind of his communion better than the few who counselled otherwise. And the event has justified his act. The whole Catholic Church has not only received the definition as certain, but acknowledged the time to be opportune. No shade of any of the anticipated dangers has been verified; but many momentous consequences to the Faith and to the Church have followed in this pontifical act. Inasmuch as those who are out of the unity of the Church lament over the Immaculate Conception as a stumbling-block in their own way, and a source of unknown evils to come hereafter to us, it may be well, at a more fitting time, to trace out the evident marks of the Divine hand in this event. We do not assume to know that which the Father has put in His own power; but, as we may know that the key which answers to the wards belongs to the lock, so when the *clavis scientiæ* corresponds minutely with the intellectual demands both of error without the Church and of truth within it, we may with certainty predicate that it is 'the Key of David' which alone 'openeth and no man shutteth, and shutteth and no man openeth.' *

We are told that the doctrine of the Immaculate Conception has no foundation in Scripture or tradition, and is contradicted by antiquity. How then is it that the whole Church, East and West, from the

* Apoc. iii. 7.

beginning, has always affirmed the Blessed Mother of God to have been sanctified with a pre-eminent and exceptional sanctification; that even those who affirm her to be of sinful flesh, *ex massa peccatrice*, affirm the same also of her Divine Son, and therefore not as affirming personal sin; that in affirming her to be free from actual sin, they affirmed by implication the absence of sin altogether; that the very term and phrase 'original sin' are technical and of western origin; that as the nature of sin was more explicitly analysed in the Pelagian controversies, she was always more explicitly excepted from all affirmation of original sin; that the fact of her sanctification does include, and not contradict, as has been most preposterously said, her Immaculate Conception, which is no more than sanctification in its sovereign fulness; that the whole Episcopate, whensoever it has approached the question, has always affirmed it; that the Councils of Ephesus and of Francfort recognised her as sinless; that the Councils of Basil and of Avignon framed decrees to declare the Immaculate Conception; that the universities of Christendom always taught it, and bound their doctors to teach it; that every great religious Order, but one, defended it; that of the one only which hesitated, a majority of its theologians, as 130 to 90, maintained it; that those who objected to the terms Immaculate Conception, held that Mary was immaculate in her nativity; that is, that she was not only free from all actual sin, but from all original sin, and that by a sanctification which preceded birth into this world; that this is the doctrine of S. Bernard, who is always made to contradict himself to serve the ends of controversy, in the very same letter to the Canons of Lyons in which he opposes their introducing, without authority of the Holy See, the Feast of the Immaculate Conception, instead of the Immaculate Nativity; that, finally, thirty-three Pontiffs, in seventy Constitutions, have protected and promoted the belief of the Immaculate Conception, on which Pius IX. did no more than impress the image and superscription of the Divine and universal tradition of the Church of God? It would have inspired more confidence in the candour and pacific aims of those who write against us, if these things had at least been recognised by so much as a statement and rejection. The case then stands thus. The pre-eminent sanctification of the Mother of God is a tradition which has descended from the earliest traceable antiquity in the universal belief or passive infallibility of the Church of God. The active infallibility of the Church, as diffused throughout the world in the Episcopate, taught it. Six times Bishops gathered in Council have implied or affirmed it. Twice they actually proposed to define it, in the very form of the Immaculate Conception; and now, lastly, the Sovereign Pontiff, after consulting the whole Episcopate throughout the world, receiving and weighing maturely the answers of some six hundred Bishops, defined the dogma *ex cathedrâ*, and the definition has been received not only with assent, but with joy, by the whole Catholic world. We have here more than a General Council, by way of protracted and universal consultation, and universal reception following. The requirements of Gallicanism are here more than satisfied. Bossuet would now judicially pronounce any man to be a heretic who should refuse to accept the Immaculate Conception as a dogma of faith. For Bossuet, in unwisely extolling General Councils above the Pope, was not unwise enough to extol them above the Church; neither was he so superficial as to believe that the Church derives its infallibility from Councils, a theory sevenfold incoherent in those who maintain that General Councils may err. He did not hold the Church to be infallible because of the infallibility of Councils; but Councils to be infallible because of the infallibility of the Church. The Church is the fountain, the Council the pool into which the supernatural gift of infallibility flows. The universal reception of the Church was to him the test of that which the universal faith or passive infallibility of the Church already believed. Council or no Council, this was to Bossuet divinely and infallibly certain. The Church diffused throughout the world is always both passively and actively infallible. Councils are accidental, not necessary, to it. The Church is a perpetual Council in itself, containing not only all that the eighteen Councils have defined, but the whole revelation of truth which can ever be defined, and the Divine discernment to define it. Bossuet held, as of faith, every Pontifical definition received by the whole Church, though no General Council had intervened. The doctrine of original sin declared by S. Innocent I., and received by the whole Church; the doctrines of grace declared in the condemnation of Baius by S. Pius V., and likewise universally received, were to him infallible utterances of the Church. The remonstrances of Pelagians in early times, and of Greeks and Protestants in his own day, were to him the voice of strangers, separate from Catholic unity, and therefore excluded from the reception of the Church. How then can those who are separated from the only Church which Bossuet recognised, say, 'We and Bossuet rest on the same foundation'?

And what is the intelligible sense of saying, that though all Churches have erred, the universal Church is infallible? What is this universal Church, and where? If the Church be divided into three parts, and each part has erred, where is the Church which cannot err? Where is it to be seen? where heard? Where does it teach? How does it witness? Whom does it govern? Who submits to it? Is it the Church before the division, or the Church after the reunion? Where, then, is it now, but in the imagination? It would seem to me that this position is of all the least tenable. It admits that the Church of God must be infallible; it rejects the exercise of its infallibility. It is, therefore, as Giraldus says, both a heresy and a treason; a treason in appealing from the ultimate sovereignty of the Church of this hour, and a heresy in denying that ultimate sovereignty to be infallible. The Church has shown its unerring instinct in rejecting all who hold this error with pertinacity.

And here we have the precise point of contact between the error of the Unionist school and the faith of the Catholic Church. The Church teaches that its infallibility, whether in or out of Council, is perpetual. The Unionist school teaches that its infallibility is intermittent, from Council to Council, and that by reason of its present divisions a General Council is impossible. The Church holds that a General Council is possible to-morrow, and that if convened and confirmed by the Sovereign Pontiff it would be infallible. But, whether a Council be held or no, the Church diffused and the Church in its Head is permanently and perpetually infallible; the ultimate and highest witness, both in the natural and supernatural order, of the original revelation, of the sense of Scripture, of the testimony of antiquity, of the mind of Councils, the supreme judge of truth and falsehood in all matters of faith and morals, and of all facts and truths in necessary contact with them. There is no obscurity as to the faith of Catholics, in relation to the Church, its nature, notes, properties, or gifts. We may be denounced as peremptory, exclusive, unreasonable; but men know what we say, because we know what we mean.

It would seem to me an unwise course for those who approach us with professions of peace and desires of reunion, to cast stones at even the least in the household of faith. It is still less wise to assail the highest and most sacred person upon earth. It is dangerous and a sign of heresy to represent the Immaculate Conception defined by the Sovereign Pontiff as a hindrance to reunion. It is dangerous also to ascribe to any man opinions visibly absurd. It is indeed true that the portion of the Catholic Church most devoted to the ' cultus ' of the Blessed Virgin is most persuaded of the personal infallibility of the Pope. But in no part of the Church, even among the most Ultramontane Catholics, is there to be found even one who believes that a continual flow of inspiration may at any time change popular opinion into infallible truth. If by this be meant into a dogma of faith, it is a simple confusion arising from want of common catechetical knowledge. No dogma is definable as of faith unless it have the first essential condition, namely, that it was revealed by God. Therefore Pius IX. in the definition of the Immaculate Conception did not declare the doctrine to be true, but to be revealed. It is hard to acquit such controversialists of a culpable want of knowledge, or of a rashness culpable in accusing.

But if this statement be intended to affirm only that popular opinion may become by the authority of the Church infallibly certain, it is most sound and

Catholic doctrine. We would give as an example of an 'infallible truth,' which was once only a popular opinion, and has become infallibly certain, though it can never become a dogma of faith, the necessity of the temporal power of the Holy See to the freedom of the Church and of its Head. It shows no exactness to impute to any one that he has made the temporal power a part of his creed.

For ourselves, Reverend and dear Brethren, it is hardly needful that I should say that as yet I have never known of any Catholic so ignorant of the Act of Faith which he learnt in childhood as to incorporate the proposition of the temporal power with the doctrines of the faith. My own mind on this subject was declared clearly enough four years ago to all who may wish to know it, or may desire not to misrepresent it. I then said:

'Inasmuch as it is better to err by excess of caution than by defect of explicitness, I will here say what I must ask all Catholics to pardon as needless to them, but necessary perhaps for those that are without.

'In the parallel I have drawn between the gradual definition of the doctrines of the Holy Trinity and of the Immaculate Conception, and the subject of the temporal power of the Sovereign Pontiffs, I have in no way and in no sense expressed or implied that the temporal power constitutes the material object of a dogma of faith.

'The first of the two conditions of a dogma of faith is, that it was revealed by God to the Apostles.

'The local sovereignty of the Vicar of our Lord over Rome and the Marches was a fact in Providence many centuries afterwards, and as such can form no proper or direct matter of a dogma of faith. The instinct of a Catholic child would perceive this; and Catholics will forgive my pointing it out only for the sake of those who either have not the light of faith, or who are given to the spirit of contention.

'Nevertheless, the temporal sovereignty affords abundant and proper matter for a definition, or judgment, or authoritative declaration of the Church, like the disciplinary decrees of General Councils; or, finally, the authoritative sentences in the Bulls of Pontiffs—as, for instance, in the Bull *Auctorem fidei*—of which many relate to discipline, to ecclesiastical and mixed questions bearing on temporal things.

'And to such an authoritative utterance, under anathema, and by the voice of the whole Church through the Supreme Pontiff, the subject of the temporal power of the Vicar of Jesus Christ may legitimately, and not improbably, attain; and such a *judicium Ecclesiæ*, or authoritative sentence, would be binding on the consciences of all the faithful, and the contrary would be noted as "propositio falsa, juribus Conciliorum Generalium et Summorum Pontificum laesiva, scandalosa et schismati fovens." And yet the subject matter may not be among the original articles of revealed doctrine, but of the nature of a dogmatic fact attaching to a Divine doctrine and institution, viz., the Vicariate of St. Peter and his successors; and therefore, after declaration, it would be of incontrovertible certainty and universal obligation, so that the denial of it would involve grave sin.'*

The necessity of the temporal power in this sense may, perhaps, be called a popular opinion until the Encyclical allocutions of the Sovereign Pontiff in 1859 and 1860. The declaration of nearly three hundred Bishops in Rome in the year 1862, and the reception of their words by the whole Episcopate of the Church, would even in Bossuet's

* 'The Temporal Power of the Vicar of Jesus Christ,' by Henry Edward Manning, D.D. Second edition, with a preface, p. xxiv.

judgment raise this opinion to the rank of a truth, which, though not a dogma of faith, is yet incontestably certain. The words of the Bishops are as follows:—' We recognise the civil princedom of the Holy See as a thing necessary, and manifestly instituted by the providence of God; nor do we hesitate to declare that in the present state of human affairs that civil princedom is required for the good and free government of the Church and of souls. For it is fitting that the Roman Pontiff, the Head of the whole Church, should be subject to no prince, nor be guest of any, but that he should dwell in his own dominions and kingdom in full personal sovereignty; and that he should protect and defend the Catholic faith, and rule and govern the whole Christian commonwealth in a dignified, tranquil, and beneficent liberty.' . . . ' But on this grave matter it hardly becomes us to say more, forasmuch as we have heard yourself not so much discoursing as teaching concerning it. For your voice has proclaimed . . . to the whole world that by "a singular counsel of the providence of God it has been ordered that the Roman Pontiff, whom Christ constituted as Head and Centre of His whole Church, should have a civil princedom." It is, therefore, to be held by us as a most certain truth, that this temporal government accrued to the Holy See not by chance, but was by a special Divine disposition conferred upon it, and by a long series of years, by an unanimous consent of kingdoms and empires, and by almost a miracle has been confirmed and preserved.'*

They who deplore Ultramontanism as a modern opinion and the extravagance of a party, must have superficially read the history of the Church, and can hardly know the one-and-twenty folio volumes of Rocaberti's 'Bibliotheca Pontificia.' And as the name of Turrecremata has been carelessly used in this sense, it may be well to hear his own words. In the year 1588, he wrote as follows: 'That See outshines others by so great a light of wisdom, that we await its teaching as divine answers from an inmost oracle. For in it, first of all, as in a resplendent fountain of light, the permanent and certain radiance of doctrine shines forth, from whence it is diffused throughout the Church for the illumination of the minds of men; for to Peter, as the head and foundation of the Church, it was specially declared, "Thou art Peter, and upon this rock I will build my Church." And again, "I have prayed for thee that thy faith fail not; and thou being once converted, confirm thy brethren." Wherefore, all who desire to cast out from their minds the anxiety of doubt, approach the Holy See as the rule of faith, and await from the Sovereign Pontiff himself, as from a heavenly authority, judgment and decision; and that because in the Roman Pontiff, as in the

* Declaration of the Bishops, &c. Acta Canonizationis Pio IX. P.P. peractæ. Rom. 1864. Pp. 544, 545.

Supreme Judge, resides the ultimate power of deciding in causes of faith, from which it was never lawful to any one to depart under pretence of appeal.' Again, he says afterwards: 'The most celebrated synods of the whole Christian world turn their eyes to him as their chiefest light, and refer the greater causes of the Church to the Bishop of Rome in person, as Christ has obtained by His prayer from the Father, that Peter, and the successor of Peter, and the Vicar of Christ himself, in pronouncing decisions of the public questions of faith, cannot err. For it was to Peter, not as a private man, but as head of the Church, and as abiding in the ecclesiastical hierarchy as long as the dominion of the Church shall endure, that it was explicitly declared, "I have prayed for thee that thy faith fail not; and thou being once converted, confirm thy brethren."'* This, at least, Turrecremata does not hold to be the language of flattery which ' equals the Popes, as it were, to God.'

It is an ill-advised overture of peace, then, to assail the popular, prevalent, and dominant opinions, devotions, and doctrines of the Catholic Church with hostile criticism, and to appeal from it to some authoritative censure to be hereafter pronounced against them. What is this but to say, you must all come to my mind before I can unite with you? And who shall say this with modesty except he be

* Alexandri a Turre Cremensis de Fulgenti Radio Eccl. Hier. lib. v. radius xviii. : ' De Vero ac Certo Apostolicæ Sedis Oraculo.' Rocaberti, Biblioth. Pont., tom. ii.

an inspired person or an infallible judge? To claim this universal censorship in the same breath which denies the infallibility of the living Church is hardly reasonable. If *sentire cum Ecclesia* be a test of conformity to the mind of the Spirit, *Ecclesiæ dissentire* is no sign of illumination; for the presence and assistance of the Holy Ghost which secures the Church within the sphere of faith and of morals, invests it also with instincts and a discernment which preside over its worship and doctrine, its practices and customs. We may be sure that whatsoever is prevalent in the Church, under the eye of its public authority, practised by the people, and not censured by its pastors, is at least conformable to faith, and innocent as to morals. Whosoever rises up to condemn such practices and opinions, thereby convicts himself of the private spirit, which is the root of heresy.

But if it be ill-advised to assail the mind of the Church, it is still more so to oppose its visible Head. There can be no doubt that the Sovereign Pontiff has declared the same opinion as to the temporal power as that which is censured in others, and that he defined the Immaculate Conception, and that he believes in his own infallibility. If these things be our reproach, we share it with the Vicar of Jesus Christ. They are not our private opinions, nor the tenets of a school, but the mind of the Pontiff, as they were of his predecessors, as they will be of those who come after him. To appeal from the Pope to an 'Eighth' General Council of Greeks, Anglicans, and Romans, who shall put down Ultramontanism, restore the Immaculate Conception to the region of pious opinions without foundation in Scripture and antiquity, declare the Pope to be fallible, and subject to General Councils which may err, reunite Christendom on the basis of the Russian Catechism, the Thirty-nine Articles, and the decrees of Trent, interpreted not as they were intended, but by the rule of a Catholicism which the Catholic world has never known, elaborated by the criticism or illuminism of uncatholic minds nurtured in an anti-Catholic religion,—all this is to us no harbinger of unity, no voice of peace, because no sign of humility, no evidence of faith. The Holy Office, with unerring discernment, has declared that the tendency of the Association for Promoting the Reunion of Christendom is indifference; that it is an attempt to widen the unity of truth by the comprehension of those who differ. The universal Church is denounced as sectarian in these days. We are reproached for narrowness by those who would explain away the decrees of Trent, and bring them down to the Greek 'orthodoxy' and the Anglican formularies. And this, too, is narrow to those who are incorporating the Anglican religion with the semi-rationalism of Germany. Unionism is outwardly a reaction against Latitudinarianism; inwardly it promotes it. There can be but two principles and two tendencies: the one, divine faith, which perpetually expands into greater bulk, opens into fuller explicitness, ascends into a loftier stature, as, for instance, the popular 'cultus' of the Mother of God, and the dominant faith of the infallibility of the Church, which rest upon the decrees of Trent, as I have said, like the cedar upon its root; the other, of human criticism, disguise it as you may in texts of Scripture, or in patristic learning, or in sceptical history, or rationalistic interpretation, the tendency of which is always to wider formulas and diminished truth, to comprehension of communion, and loss of faith. There can be no doubt that the peril of the next ten years will be latitudinarian Christianity in all its forms. So long as men are approaching to the Catholic Church they hold the necessity of precise and inflexible dogma. The moment they waver in their approach, fidelity to dogma declines; they then feel about for a new basis. As it cannot be precision, it must be vagueness. Dogma is against them; they must be against dogma. Theology excludes them; they must hold theology cheap. From that moment (we write what we have seen) men move off from the path of truth, insensibly for awhile, unconsciously to themselves. The Catholic faith is 'Latin Christianity;' the Catholic Church is Rome; Trent is occidental; theology a transient phase of mediæval thought; Christianity the education of the world, the joint contribution of nations, wide as the human race, old as creation, intolerant of visible forms, impatient of mixture with the earthly elements of government and temporal power, purer than the Church of God, awaiting its redemption from the bigotries of sects and churches, its investiture in the theology of the nineteenth century, and the Church of the future. Such is the tendency of the day of which the theory of union before truth is the one extreme, and the rationalism of freemasonry is the other. All other forms of thought are but intermediates, one in principle, all alike irreconcilable with the principles of Divine faith, the presence of a Divine Teacher, and unconditional submission to His voice.

In your dealings, then, with persons of these opinions, Reverend Brethren, you will keep steadfastly to one point, namely, the perpetual infallibility of the Church, whether diffused, or in Council, whether speaking by the Council of Trent or by its Head. It is necessary to be on your guard against two modes of argument by which this affirmation is evaded. The one is to lead away into details, such as the devotion to the Blessed Virgin, or the Temporal Power of the Pope. This has the effect of diversion, and the main issue is left without an answer. The other is to admit the perpetual Divine office of the Church, denying the infallibility of its Head, and of the Councils held since the schism of the Greek Church. The sure test of this is to ask, Do you believe in the infallibility of the Council of Trent? Do you believe the Pontifical declarations of doctrine since the Council of Trent, received as they are also by the Catholic Church, to be infallible? If the answer be Yes, you will know how to proceed. If it be No, you will have the proof that this supposed perpetual office or infallibility of the Church is a private imagination, like the doctrine of consubstantiation, or of particular redemption, or of divided unity.

Another test by which the absence of real faith or of real knowledge respecting the Divine office of the Church may be detected, is the objection which is made to the alleged definitions of new doctrine, and the making them the new terms of communion. If the Church be fallible, then such new definitions may, and in all probability would be, human opinions, and to make them articles of faith and communion would be tyrannous and schismatical. A supreme power claiming to regulate the faith and conscience of men, if liable to error, is an usurpation and a despotism. None would deprecate and abjure such new definitions so inflexibly as Catholics. They died rather than accept them under Henry VIII. and Queen Elizabeth.

But if the authority which defines these doctrines have a Divine assistance to preserve it from error, every new definition is a new declaration of truth, a broader light, and a more perfect knowledge of the Revelation of God. To object to such accessions of knowledge, proves that the Divine source and certainty of them is denied; for no man of sound or pious mind would deprecate a clearer and more perfect knowledge of the mind of God. It would be like saying, 'Let the Holy One of Israel cease from before us.'* When these men desire to stay the onward course and growth of the living Church, and to keep down the explicit mind of the Church to a minimum as a means of reunion with their maximum—a strange dialect in matters of faith—as it is impossible, without great severity of judgment upon them, to imagine that they wish to bind the operations of the Holy Spirit, or to refuse His perpetual voice, it is evident that they deny His presence and His operations in the perpetual office of the Church. But this is what we affirmed and they denied from the beginning.

An impartial critic, further from the Catholic Church than from Anglicanism, well observed, that it is strange for men who proclaim so constraining a desire for unity to keep open a separation, for the difference between a maximum and a minimum which is supposed to be almost coincident. The critic further adds with great perspicuity, that the question of a little more or a little less of dogma can be nothing to those who accept the principle of infallibility, and that to those who do not accept it, there is no question of more or less.

I cannot refrain from noticing a letter lately published with the signature of Prince Orloff,† the Russian Minister at the Court of Brussels, detailing

---

* Isaias xxx. 11.
† 'Times' newspaper, Dec. 28, 1865.

the discussions held at a meeting on the 15th of November last, at which certain Anglican Bishops and ' about eighty persons, chiefly clergymen of High Church principles,' were assembled for the purpose of promoting union with the Russo-Greek Church. I notice it only to draw out certain points in confirmation of what has been hitherto said.

First, it is evident that if the Anglican clergy there present are willing to unite with the Russian Greeks, the mass of the Anglican Church and of the English people have no such will. Out of this project of union a domestic disunion of the gravest kind at once arises.

Next, it is equally certain, by the steady refusal of the Greeks to communicate with the Protestant or Reformed bodies, expressed again and again, as is the case in the seventeenth century of Cyril Leuchar, and in the overtures of Dr. Basire, and lately of Mr. William Palmer, and of the Anglican clergyman who went the other day to Servia, and most transparently shown in the conduct of Prince Orloff, detailed in his letter, that the Greek Church absolutely refuses all contact with those who are out of its communion, and at variance with its traditional ' Orthodoxy,' in which the Seven Sacraments, and the honour due to the Mother of God are primary and essential points.

Again, there is but little reliance to be placed in the professions of desire of reunion with Rome, when at the same time they who make them are courting union with those who for a thousand years have made animosity to Rome a test of fidelity to Constantinople.

But, lastly, the strangest revelation in this affair was the proposal of instant communion, despite of all differences of doctrine or of faith. Prince Orloff wisely proposed that truth should prepare the way for unity. But this slow process was too tardy for some who were present. They proposed immediate communion in the Lord's Supper, postponing the adjustment of doctrinal differences; urging that 'we should not content ourselves with preparing the ground, leaving the harvest to be reaped by future generations, but deferring all dogmatical debates, proceed to celebrate the Lord's Supper by intercommunion.' The Holy Office was not wrong, therefore, in pronouncing that Unionism implies indifferentism. The comments which these proceedings have elicited both in England and Scotland, show how little this country is disposed for any such enterprises, and how impracticable and unreal it holds them.

These things we have written, Reverend and dear Brethren, under a constraining sense of duty towards our Divine Master, and the souls of our brethren in separation. God knows that the desire of our hearts and prayer to God is that they may be saved. If our life would reconcile this land, which we love so well, to the unity of the faith and of the Church, we trust that life would not be dear. But truth is better than life; and truth alone can restore us to unity. 'I am the way, the truth, and the life; no man cometh unto the Father but by me.'* Compromise, concession, conditions, transactions, explanations which soften Divine decrees, and evade the precision of infallible declarations of the Church, are not inspirations of the Holy Ghost. To hold out hopes of impossible events is deception and cruelty. A true love of souls dictates another course. Clear, open, patient, loving exhortations, definite and precise declarations of truth, without sharpness, and without controversy; holding up the light of faith, which by a sacramental power of its own enters into men and illuminates them when they are least aware; confidence in the supernatural grace, and the divine mission of the Church, in its authority to teach and its power to save—these are our nets to let down into the sea, our sickles to reap in the Master's field. We are put in charge with the whole Revelation of God, and of all the souls around us. We must labour for them, though they smite us. We must 'gladly spend, and be spent for them; although loving them more, we be loved less.'† Jesus did not lift a hand to shadow His face from the shame and spitting; not even to ward the blow from His cheek, much less to return the buffet which smote Him on the mouth. We have greater things at stake; nobler things in charge. We are guardians of the unity of the Truth, of the purity of the fold, of the infallible rule of faith, of the sovereign jurisdiction of Jesus Christ. We speak

---

* S. John, xiv. 6.   † 2 Cor. xii. 15.

in the name of the universal Church of God, which is the same in every place, and even by us here, in our fewness and weakness, speaks with the voice of the Church throughout the world, binds and looses with the keys of the kingdom of heaven. We received them from the Vicar of Christ; he from the Son of God. We cannot open or shut but as He wills. If we close the door to those who approach it as critics, teachers, and reformers, it is for their sakes, that one day we may open it wide, with joy and thanksgiving, when they shall have learned to know its voice to be the voice of the Son of God. 'Therefore let Christ speak, because in Christ the Church speaks, and in the Church Christ speaks; both the body in the Head, and the Head in the body.* And in the day when this is known, they will see that we have not been uncharitable, narrow or exclusive; but that they have thought to stay up the ark by laying their hands upon it. The Church of God accepts of no support, or service, except from its own divine power and commission: and truth can be spread in no way but that which our Lord has consecrated. 'If any man would be My disciple, let him take up his cross and follow Me.' He called men one by one. He so calls them still.

It is not for us to ask, 'Lord, what shall this man do?' The voice of Truth is articulate and clear, 'Follow thou me.' To question about others is to forget

---

* S. Aug. in Psalm. xl. tom. iv. p. 344.

ourselves. To check our own convictions is to resist a Divine grace. To wait for others is to assume a control over the dispensations of the Spirit. God calls whom, and as, and when He wills. We shall die alone, and be judged one by one. It is, therefore, by the obedience of the whole soul, all alone with God, detached from kindred and home, from all human traditions, from even spiritual bonds, by the witness of our whole being, at all costs and sorrows, by sufferings for the Truth, and that to the apparent overthrow of the work of a life, and the forfeiture of all usefulness to come; it is only by this that we can testify to the faith and make men believe it to be true, and believe that we believe it ourselves. So our Divine Master witnessed 'a good confession,' and so His disciples in every time and land have obeyed the Spirit of Truth, and won souls from error. It is not by movements like this, nor by convictions merged in parties, that truth is served and souls saved. Much less is it so that schism can be healed, or errors cast out. The act of conforming our own intelligence to the truth, and our own will to obedience, is the highest, the most divine, the only way in which we can promote the unity of the Church and the supremacy of faith. And this we shall do all the more powerfully and deeply in proportion as we suffer for it, and suffer, if so it be, one by one. I cannot doubt that of those who have addressed the Holy Office, and of those who are united in this movement, there are many who sincerely desire to be reunited to the Apostolic See, the mother of all churches, and believe that they are advancing to this end. They have a zeal of God, but not according to knowledge. 'Magni passus,' as S. Augustin says, 'sed extra viam.' So far as this movement shall lead to the submission of individuals to the truth, it is of God; so far as it leads to the suppression of individual convictions and individual responsibility, it is not of God.

And now it is more than time to make an end.

Thus far I have been constrained by the imperative law of truth to lay bare the impossibility and the unlawfulness of all union except that which is based upon the only and infallible Church of God. 'Other foundation can no man lay than that which is laid.'* Nothing else will endure the day of His judgment. All other work will be burnt up. But I cannot so dismiss the thought of union; the vision, distant as it may be, of seeing my brethren, countrymen, friends, and kinsmen once more in the bond of peace, of kneeling with them once before I die in the presence of Jesus upon the altar. God knows that for this I have prayed and laboured; for this I have incurred their displeasure and borne many a wound. For this I am ready to bear much more, and to bear it to the end. Every affection of nature and of grace binds me to desire, next after the glory of God, their salvation and the conversion of

---

* 1 Cor. iii. 11.

England. To this I gladly give the few years that remain to me in life. I know what it will cost me by what it has cost me already. 'Am I become your enemy because I tell you the truth?' But truth unites or divides. It is never neutral; it never returns void. It kindles charity or enmity, and is 'a sweet odour of Christ unto God, both in them that are saved and in them that perish: to the one the odour of life unto life; to the other, of death unto death; and for these things who is sufficient?'*

The Holy Office concludes its letter with words full of charity, calling on those who addressed it to return into the bosom of the One only Church which from its intrinsic nature can never be divided. It assures them that the Sovereign Pontiff with all his heart implores this grace for them continually from the Father of Light and of all Mercy. To this prevailing prayer let us add our own daily supplications, that the Spirit of Unity and Truth will out of the darkness of our country show to all men His marvellous light, and out of the confusions of this moment, and in the midst of the faults of men, call forth once more a new creation of unity in truth. And for this the prayers of saints and martyrs are ascending, and, above all, the prayers of those whose tears and whose blood have sunk into the soil of England. They so loved unity that they died for it; they so loved truth that they laid down their lives for its

* 2 Cor. ii. 15, 16.

sake. Their tears and their blood have not been shed in vain. They are ascending up before God with the intercession of His Immaculate Mother for the land which has so long forgotten to call her blessed. I might say more, but I refrain. Grant this, O Lord, in thine own good time and way, for the souls so dear to us are dearer still to Thee, for Thou hast redeemed them in Thy most precious blood.

I remain, Reverend and dear Brethren,

Your affectionate Servant in Christ,

✠ HENRY EDWARD,
ARCHBISHOP OF WESTMINSTER.

Epiphany 1866.

APPENDIX.

I.

A Letter of the Supreme Holy Roman and Universal Inquisition to all the English Bishops.

It has been notified to the Apostolic See that some Catholics and even ecclesiastics have given their names to a Society established in London in the year 1857, ' for promoting' (as it is called) ' the unity of Christendom;' and that several articles have been published in the daily papers signed with the names of Catholics, in approval of this Society, or supposed to have been written by ecclesiastics in its favour. Now, the real character and aim of the Society are plain, not only from the articles in the journal called the ' Union Review,' but from the very prospectus in which persons are invited to join it, and are enrolled as members. Organised and conducted by Protestants, it has resulted from a view, put forth by it in express terms, that the three Christian communions, the Roman Catholic, the schismatic Greek, and the Anglican, though separated and divided one from another, have yet an equal claim to the title of Catholic. Hence, its doors are open to all men whencesoever—Catholics, schismatic Greeks, or Anglicans—but so that none shall moot the question of the several points of doctrine in which they differ, and each may follow undisturbed the opinions of his own religious profession. It appoints, moreover, prayers to be said by all its members, and Masses to be celebrated by priests, according to its particular intention; namely, that these three Christian communions, constituting, as by hypothesis they do, the Catholic Church collectively, may at some future time coalesce to the formation of one body.

The Supreme Congregation of the Holy Office, to whose scrutiny the matter has been referred as usual, has judged, after mature consideration, that the faithful should be warned with all care against being led by heretics to join with them and with schismatics in entering this Association. The Most Eminent Fathers the Cardinals, placed with myself over the Sacred Inquisition, entertain, indeed, no doubt that the Bishops of those parts address themselves already with diligence, according to the charity and learning which distinguish them, to point out the evils which that Association diffuses, and to repel the dangers it is bringing on. Yet they would seem wanting to their office, did they not, in a matter of such moment, further enkindle the said Bishops' pastoral zeal; this novelty being all the more perilous as it bears a semblance of religion, and of being much concerned for the unity of the Christian society.

The principle on which it rests is one that overthrows the divine constitution of the Church. For it is pervaded by the idea that the true Church of Jesus Christ consists partly of the Roman Church spread abroad and propagated throughout the world, partly of the Photian schism and the Anglican heresy, as having equally with the Roman Church, one Lord, *one faith*, and one baptism. To take away the dissensions which distract these three Christian communions, not without grievous scandal and at the expense of truth and charity, it appoints prayers and sacrifices, to obtain from God the grace of unity. Nothing indeed should be dearer to a Catholic than the eradicating of schisms and dissensions among Christians, and to see all Christians '*solicitous to keep the unity of the Spirit in the bond of peace*' (Eph. iv.). To that end, the Catholic Church offers prayers to Almighty God, and urges the faithful in Christ to pray, that all who have left the Holy Roman Church, out of which is no salvation, may abjure their errors and be brought to the true faith, and the peace of that Church; nay, that all men may, by God's merciful aid, attain to a knowledge of the truth. But that the faithful in Christ, and that ecclesiastics, should pray for Christian unity under the direction of heretics, and, worse still, according to an intention stained and infected by heresy in a high degree, can no way be tolerated. The true Church of Jesus Christ is constituted and recognised as such by those four 'notes,' belief in which is asserted in the Creed, each note being so linked with the rest as to be incapable of separation. Hence, the Church Catholic, truly so called, must be luminous with all the high attributes of unity, sanctity, and apostolical succession. The Catholic Church therefore is One, in the manifest and perfect unity of all nations of the world; that is, the unity of which the supreme authority and more eminent principality of blessed Peter, Prince of the Apostles, and his successors in the Roman See is the principle, the root, and indefectible origin. She is no other than that Church which, built on Peter alone, grows up into one body knit together and compacted in unity of faith and charity; which blessed Cyprian in his 45th Epistle heartily acknowledged, where he addresses Pope Cornelius: 'that our colleagues may firmly approve and hold to thee and thy communion—that is, alike to the unity and charity of the Catholic Church.' It was the assertion of this same truth that Pope Hormisdas required of the bishops who abjured the schism of Acacius, in the formula approved by the suffrage of all Christian antiquity, in which they 'who agree not in all things with the Apostolic See' are said to be 'put forth from the communion of the Church Catholic.' So far from its being possible that communions separate from the Roman See can be rightly called or reputed Catholic, their very separation and disagreement is the mark by which to know those communities and Christians that hold neither the true faith, nor the true doctrine of Christ, as Irenæus (lib. iii. *contra Hæres.* c. 3) most clearly showed as early as the second century. Let the faithful, then, jealously beware of joining those societies to which they cannot unite themselves and yet keep their faith unimpaired; and listen to S. Augustine, who teaches that there can be neither truth nor piety where Christian unity and the charity of the Holy Spirit are absent.

A further reason why the faithful ought to keep themselves entirely apart from the London Society is this, that they who unite in it both favour *indifferentism* and introduce scandal. That Society, at least its founders and directors, assert that Photianism and Anglicanism are two forms of one true Christian religion, in which the same means of pleasing God are afforded as in the Catholic Church; and that the active dissensions in which these Christian communions exist, are short of any breach of the faith, inasmuch as their faith continues one and the same. Yet this is the very essence of that most baleful indifference in matters of religion, which is at this time especially spreading in secret with the greatest injury to souls. Hence no proof is needed that Catholics who join this Society are giving both to Catholics and non-Catholics an occasion of spiritual ruin: more especially because the Society, by holding out a vain expectation of those three communions, each in its integrity, and keeping each to its own persuasion, coalescing in one, leads the minds of non-Catholics away from conversion to the faith, and, by the journals it publishes, endeavours to prevent it.

The most anxious care, then, is to be exercised, that no Catholics may be deluded either by appearance of piety or by unsound opinions, to join or in any way favour the Society in question, or any similar one; that they may not be carried away, by a delusive yearning for such new-fangled Christian unity, into a fall from that perfect unity which by a wonderful gift of Divine grace stands on the firm foundation of Peter.

C. CARD. PATRIZI.

Rome, this 16th day of September, 1864.

II.

ADDRESS FROM ANGLICAN CLERGY TO CARDINAL PATRIZI.

To the Most Eminent and Most Reverend Father in Christ, and Lord C. Cardinal Patrizi, Prefect of the Sacred Office.

MOST EMINENT LORD,

We the undersigned Deans, Canons, Parish Priests, and other Priests of the Anglo-Catholic Church, earnestly desiring the visible reunion, according to the will of our Lord, of the several parts of the Christian family, have read with great regret your Eminence's letter 'To all the English Bishops.'

In that letter, our Society, instituted to promote the Reunion of all Christendom, is charged with affirming in its prospectus, that 'the three Communions, the Roman Catholic, the Eastern, and the Anglican, have an equal claim to call themselves Catholic.'

On that question our prospectus gave no opinion whatever. What we said, treated of the question of *fact*, not of *right*. We merely affirmed that the Anglican Church claimed the name Catholic; as is abundantly plain to all, both from the Liturgy and the Articles of Religion.

Moreover, as to the intention of our Society, that letter asserts our especial aim to be, 'that the three Communions named, each in its integrity, and each maintaining still its own opinions, may coalesce into one.'

Far from us and from our Society be such an aim as this; from which were to be anticipated, not ecclesiastical unity, but merely a discord of brethren in personal conflict under one roof. What we beseech Almighty God to grant, and desire with all our hearts, is simply that œcumenical intercommunion which existed before the separation of East and West, founded and consolidated on the profession of one and the same Catholic faith.

Moreover, the Society aforesaid should all the less excite your jealousy, that it abstains from action, and simply prays, in the words of Christ our Lord, 'May there be one Fold and one Shepherd.' This alone finds place in our hearts' desire; and this is the principle and the yearning we express to your Eminence with the utmost earnestness, with sincere heart and voice unfeigned.

As to the journal entitled 'The Union Review,' the connection between it and the Society is purely accidental, and we are therefore in no way pledged to its *dicta*. In that little work various writers put forth indeed their own opinions, but only to the further elucidation of the truth of the Catholic Faith by developing them. That such a mode of contributing papers should not be in use in Rome, where the controversies of the day are seldom under discussion, is hardly to be wondered at; but in England, where almost every question becomes public property, none results in successful conviction without free discussion.

To hasten this event, we have now laboured during many years. We have effected improvements, beyond what could be hoped for, where the faith of the flock, or divine worship, or clerical discipline, may have been imperfect: and, not to be deemed forgetful of others, we have cultivated a feeling of good will towards the venerable Church of Rome, that has for a long time caused some to mistrust us.

We humbly profess ourselves your Eminence's servants, devoted to Catholic unity.

(This Address was signed by 198 Clergy of the Church of England.)

III.

ANSWER OF HIS EMINENCE CARDINAL PATRIZI TO THE FOREGOING LETTER.

HONOURED AND VERY DEAR SIRS,

In the letter you have sent me, you profess as your only desire, with sincere heart and voice unfeigned, that, in our Lord's words, there should be one fold and one shepherd. This gives the Sacred Congregation a pleasing hope of your finally attaining to true unity, through the Divine grace of our Lord Jesus Christ. But you must beware lest, in seeking it, you turn aside from the way. It causes the Sacred Congregation the most heartfelt sorrow that such has been your case; forasmuch as you imagine that those Christian communities which claim to have inherited the priesthood and the name Catholic, constitute portions of the true Church of Jesus Christ, though divided and separated from the Apostolic See of Peter. Nothing is more contrary to the true idea of the Catholic Church than such a notion. For, as my letter to the English Bishops lays down, that is the Catholic Church which, built on Peter alone, grows up into one body, knit together and compacted in the unity of faith and charity.* If, indeed, you will examine the matter with care, and dispassionately consider it, evident proofs will show that this unity of faith and charity—that is, of communion—is, by the immutable institution of Christ, not only a chief and fundamental attribute of the Church, but a note, sure and ever visible, whereby the Church herself is, with security and ease, distinguishable from all sects. Witness the express affirmations, the definite metaphors, the parables and similitudes of the sacred Scriptures, portraying, as it were, the Church in outline; then, the plain documents of the holy Fathers and Councils; again, the uniform method which the Church has from the first adopted against heretics and schismatics of every race, many of whom, all the while, arrogated to themselves the priesthood and the name Catholic. As, then, the Church of Christ is Catholic, and is called so, by virtue of that supreme unity of faith and communion which, diffused as she is through all nations and all time, she still firmly maintains; so, in virtue of that same unity, is she entitled Holy and Apostolic; and as without such unity she would cease, *de jure* and *de facto*, to be Catholic, so would she at once lose the attributes of sanctity and apostolical succession.

Its unity, however, the Church of Christ never has

---

* S. Ambros. de Offic. Ministr. lib. iii. c. 3, n. 19.

lost; never, for the briefest interval of time, will lose: forasmuch as, by the divine oracles, the Church is to endure for ever. But how can its perpetual duration be believed, if the succession of ages bring about new aspects and form in its essential condition, even as in the changeful things of this world; and if the Church itself could at any time lapse so far from that unity of faith and communion in which it was founded by Jesus Christ and then propagated by the Apostles? For therefore, says S. Ambrose, will the reign of the Church endure for ever, because the faith is undivided and the body one.* Now, if the Church of Christ be altogether indefectible, it follows at once that it is to be asserted and believed infallible also in propounding the doctrines of the Gospel. And that Christ our Lord, by a wonderful gift, has bestowed on His Church, of which He is Himself the Head, the Bridegroom, and the Corner Stone, this prerogative of infallibility, is a fixed dogma of the Catholic faith. What man of sound mind, indeed, could persuade himself that error might lurk in the Church's public and authoritative office as teacher, instituted by Christ to this very end, that we should not now be children, tossed to and fro, and carried about with every wind of doctrine, in the wickedness of men, in craftiness by which they lie in wait to deceive; † which He promised should never be destitute of His own presence, and should be taught all truth by the Holy Ghost;

---

* In Luc. lib. vii. n. 91.   † Ephes. iv. 14.

through which He willed that all nations should be called to the obedience of faith, and be taught what to believe, and what to do; so that he should be condemned who would not believe the preaching of the Apostles and their lawful successors; and to which He gave the function and authority to prescribe the form of sound words, wherein all who are taught of God should unite? Hence S. Paul calls the Church the pillar and ground of the truth.* But how could the Church be the ground of the truth, unless they who sought were secure of obtaining the truth at her hands? Moreover, the holy Fathers, speaking with one voice, proclaim that the unity of the faith and doctrine of Christ is so inherent in the unity of the Church that the one cannot be disjoined from the other; which is the meaning of that golden saying of S. Cyprian, that the Church is the home of unity and truth.† Nor has the Catholic Church been ever in doubt of this prerogative, promised and communicated to it by the continual presence of Christ and the assistance of the Holy Ghost, so often as it has applied itself to decide controversies which arise on faith, to interpret the sacred Scriptures, or to overthrow such errors as oppose the deposit of revelation committed to it. It has ever put forth and proposed its definitions of dogma as a certain and immutable rule of faith, every one being bound to yield to them in-

---

* 1 Timoth. iii. 15.
† Epist. viii. ad Cornel. ap. Coustant, n. 1.

terior assent, without doubtfulness, uncertainty, or hesitation, as to a rule of faith. And such as contumaciously resist these definitions would, by the very fact, be judged to have made shipwreck of the faith necessary to salvation, and ceased to belong to Christ's flock. All which brings out more and more the absurdity of that figment of a Catholic Church as a coalition of three communions; a figment whose authors are of necessity driven to deny the Church's infallibility.

Quite as certain is the proof that Christ Jesus, in order to produce and ever preserve unity in His Church, and through the appointment of a head to remove all occasion of schism,* has, by a special providence, chosen the most blessed Peter in preference to the other Apostles, to be their Prince, and the conspicuous centre and bond of that unity. On him He has built His Church; to him He has given supreme charge and authority to feed the entire flock, to confirm his brethren, to bind and to loose throughout the world; continuing it to his successors in every age. A Catholic dogma is one which, coming from the lips of Christ, delivered and maintained by the perpetual teaching of the Fathers, has been religiously preserved by the universal Church through every age, and which it has often confirmed against the errors of innovators, by decrees of supreme Pontiffs and Councils. Hence, that alone has ever been

* S. Hieronym. lib. i. adv. Jovin. n. 26.

believed to be the Church Catholic which is united in faith and communion with the See of the Roman Pontiffs, successors of Peter; the See named, therefore, by S. Cyprian the root and matrix of the Catholic Church,* designated by Fathers and Councils, as its especial title, the Apostolic See; the See whence sacerdotal unity took its rise;† whence the laws of religious communion flow to all;‡ wherein Peter ever lives, presides, and holds out to all who seek the truths of faith.§ S. Augustine, as we know, when he would recall the Donatists, convicted of schism, to the root and the vine whence they had departed, uses an argument frequent also with the earlier Fathers: 'Come, my brethren, if ye would be grafted into the Vine. It is grievous to see you cut off and lying there. Number up the priests from the See of Peter itself, and see who in that series of Fathers succeeded to whom. That is the Rock, against which the haughty gates of hell prevail not.'∥

No other proof is needed that he is not in the Catholic Church who is not joined to that Rock on which the foundation of Catholic unity is laid. In the same sense, S. Jerome held every one to be profane who was not united in communion with the

---

* Epist. iv. ad Cornel. ap. Coustant, n. 3.

† S. Cypr. epist. xii. ad Cornel. ap. Coustant, n. 11.

‡ Epist. Conc. Aquil. ad Gratian. Imp. an. 381, inter epist. S. Ambrosii.

§ S. Pet. Chrysol. epist. ad Eutych. Act. iii. Concil. Ephes. ap. Harduin, i. 1478.

∥ Psalm. in part. Donati.

See of Peter and the Pontiff seated there. 'Following (he writes to Damasus) no chief but Christ, I am joined in communion with your holiness, that is, with the chair of Peter. On that rock I know that the Church is built. Whosoever eateth the Lamb out of this house is profane. If any one be not in the ark of Noe he will perish when the flood prevails. Whosoever gathereth not with thee, scattereth; that is, he who is not of Christ is of Antichrist.'* In the same sense, also, S. Optatus of Milevis proclaims that chair to be one, known to all, set up in Rome, in which unity is so to be preserved by all that he is a schismatic and heretic whosoever sets up any other chair against that one alone.† And rightly too; for, as S. Irenæus openly proclaims to all, in the ordination and succession of the Roman Pontiffs, the tradition and publication of truth in the Church, which began with the Apostles, has come down even to us; this being proof complete that one and the same lifegiving faith in the Church is handed down and preserved in truth from the Apostles to this day.‡

If, then, it be a mark of Christ's Church, special and perpetual, that with perfect unity in faith and charity of communion, it coheres, flourishes, and, as a city set on a hill, is manifest to all men in all time; if, again, Christ has willed that of such unity the Apostolic See of Peter should be the source, the

---

* Epist. xiv. al. 57, ad Damas. n. 2.
† De Schism. Donatist. lib. ii. n. 2.
‡ Lib. iii. contra Hæres. c. 3, n. 3, ex vet. interpret.

centre, and the bond, it follows that no congregation whatsoever, separated from the external visible communion and obedience of the Roman Pontiff, can be the Church of Christ, or can in any way whatsoever belong to the Church of Christ: to that Church which, after the Holy Trinity, is proposed to our belief in the Creed as a Church Holy, One, True, Catholic;* called Catholic not only by its children, but by all its enemies beside;† with such exclusive possession of the name that, whereas all heretics claim to be called Catholics, yet if a stranger should ask where the Catholic Church assembles, no heretic ventures to point out his own temple or place of meeting.‡ It cannot belong to that Church by means of which, as by a body in intimate union with Himself, Christ bestows the benefits of His redemption; severed from which, however much one may hold himself to be living blamelessly, yet for this sin alone, of being disjoined from the unity of Christ, he shall not have life, but the wrath of God remaineth on him.§ Wherefore, as the name Catholic can by no manner of right belong to such communions, so can it in no way be given to them without manifest heresy.

From all which, honoured and very dear Sirs, you will see why this Sacred Congregation has so care-

---

* S. Aug. de Symbol. ad Catech. c. vi.
† S. Aug. de Verâ Relig. c. vii.
‡ S. Aug. contra Epist. Fundam. c. iv. n. 5.
§ S. Aug ep. cxli. al. 152, n. 5.'

fully provided against the faithful of Christ being permitted to enrol themselves in, or to favour in any way, the Society you have lately set on foot to promote (as you express it) the unity of Christendom. You will also see that every effort at reconciliation must needs be in vain, except on condition of those principles on which the Church was at first founded by Christ, and thenceforward in every succeeding age propagated one and the same throughout the world by the Apostles and their successors; principles clearly expressed in that well-known formula of Hormisdas, which has been approved beyond all question by the whole Catholic Church. Lastly, you will see that the universal intercommunion before the Photian schism, of which you speak, obtained because at that time the Eastern Churches had not fallen away from the submission due to the Apostolic See; and that to restore such intercommunion, so greatly to be desired, it will not suffice that ill-will and hatred to the Roman Church be laid aside, but, by the precept and appointment of Christ, and by an absolute necessity, the faith and communion of the Roman Church be accepted; since, in the words of your illustrious countryman, Venerable Bede, 'Whosoever they be who in any way withdraw from the unity of the faith, or from communion with him (blessed Peter), these can neither be absolved from the bonds of their sins, nor enter the gate of the heavenly kingdom.'*

---

* Hom. in Nat. SS. Petri et Pauli.

Seeing, then, honoured and very dear Sirs, that *the Catholic Church has been shown to be one, and incapable of partition or division,** we would have you hesitate no longer to take refuge in the bosom of that Church which, by acknowledgment of all mankind, holds the supreme authority by the succession of its Bishops from the Apostolic See; heretics contending against it in vain.† May the Holy Spirit vouchsafe to fulfil and perfect without delay what He has begun in you by that good will towards the Church which He has imparted to you. And this, in union with the Sacred Congregation, our most holy Lord Pope Pius IX. desires with all his heart; and earnestly beseeches from the God of mercies and Father of lights that all of you at length, escaping from your severed, disinherited condition into the inheritance of Christ, the true Catholic Church, to which unquestionably your forefathers belonged before the deplorable separation of the sixteenth century, may happily attain the root of charity in the bond of peace and fellowship of unity.‡ Farewell.

C. CARD. PATRIZI.

Rome, this 8th November, 1865.

* S. Cypr. ep. viii. ad Cornel. ap. Coustant, n. 2.
† S. Aug. de Utilit. Credendi, c. xvii. n. 35.
‡ S. Aug. ep. lxi. al. 223, n. 2 ; ep. lxix. al. 238, n. 1.

IV.

Supremae S. Romanae et Universalis Inquisitionis Epistola ad omnes Angliae Episcopos.

APOSTOLICAE Sedi nuntiatum est, catholicos nonnullos et ecclesiasticos quoque viros Societati *ad procurandam*, uti aiunt, *Christianitatis unitatem* Londini anno 1857 erectae, nomen dedisse, et jam plures evulgatos esse ephemeridum articulos, qui catholicorum huic Societati plaudentium nomine inscribuntur, vel ab ecclesiasticis viris eamdem Societatem commendantibus exarati perhibentur. Et sane quaenam sit hujus Societatis indoles vel quo ea spectet, nedum ex articulis ephemeridis cui titulus ' *The Union Review*,' sed ex ipso folio quo socii invitantur et adscribuntur, facile intelligitur. A protestantibus quippe efformata et directa eo excitata est spiritu, quem expresse profitetur, tres videlicet Christianas communiones Romano-catholicam, Graeco-schismaticam et Anglicanam, quamvis invicem separatas ac divisas, aequo tamen jure catholicum nomen sibi vindicare. Aditus igitur in illam patet omnibus ubique locorum degentibus tum Catholicis, tum Graeco-schismaticis, tum Anglicanis, ea tamen lege ut nemini liceat de variis doctrinae capitibus in quibus dissentiunt quaestionem movere, et singulis fas sit propriae religiosae confessionis placita tranquillo animo sectari. Sociis vero omnibus preces ipsa recitandas, et sacerdotibus Sacrificia celebranda indicit juxta suam intentionem: ut nempe tres memoratae christianae communiones, utpote quae, prout supponitur, Ecclesiam Catholicam omnes simul jam constituunt, ad unum corpus efformandum tandem aliquando coeant.

Suprema S. O. Congregatio, ad cujus examen hoc negotium de more delatum est, re mature perpensa, necessarium judicavit sedulam ponendam esse operam, ut edoceantur fideles ne haereticorum ductu hanc cum iisdem haereticis et schismaticis societatem ineant. Non dubitant profecto Emi Patres Cardinales una mecum praepositi Sacrae Inquisitioni, quin istius regionis Episcopi pro ea, qua eminent, caritate et doctrina omnem jam adhibeant diligentiam ad vitia demonstranda, quibus ista Societas scatet, et ad propulsanda quae secum affert pericula: nihilominus muneri suo deesse viderentur, si pastoralem eorumdem Episcoporum zelum in re adeo gravi vehementius non inflammarent: eo enim periculosior est haec novitas, quo ad speciem pia et de christianae societatis unitate admodum sollicita videtur.

Fundamentum cui ipsa innititur hujusmodi est quod divinam Ecclesiae constitutionem susque deque vertit. Tota enim in eo est, ut supponat veram Jesu Christi Ecclesiam coustare partim ex Romana Ecclesia per universum orbem diffusa et propagata, partim vero ex schismate Photiano et ex Anglicana haeresi, quibus aeque ac Ecclesiae Romanae unus sit Dominus, *una fides* et unum baptisma. Ad removendas vero dissensiones, quibus hae tres christianae communiones cum gravi scandalo et cum veritatis et caritatis dispendio divexantur, preces et sacrificia indicit, ut a Deo gratia unitatis impetretur. Nihil certe viro Catholico potius esse debet, quam ut inter Christianos schismata et dissensiones a radice evellantur, et Christiani omnes sint *solliciti servare unitatem spiritus in vinculo pacis* (Ephes. iv.). Quapropter Ecclesia Catholica preces Deo O. M. fundit et Christifideles ad orandum excitat, ut ad veram fidem convertantur et in gratiam cum Sancta Romana Ecclesia, extra quam non est salus, ejuratis erroribus, restituantur quicumque omnes ab eadem Ecclesia recesserunt: imo ut omnes homines ad agnitionem veritatis, Deo bene juvante, perveniant. At quod Christifideles et ecclesiastici viri haereticorum ductu, et quod pejus est, juxta intentionem haeresi quammaxime pollutam et infectam pro christiana unitate orent, tolerari nullo modo potest. Vera Jesu Christi Ecclesia quadruplici nota, quam in symbolo credendam asserimus, auctoritate divina constituitur et dignoscitur: et quaelibet ex hisce notis ita cum aliis cohaeret ut ab iis nequeat sejungi: hinc fit, ut quae vere est et dicitur Catholica, unitatis simul, sanctitatis et Apostolicae successionis praerogativa debeat effulgere. Ecclesia igitur Catholica una est unitate conspicua perfectaque orbis terrae et omnium gentium, ea profecto unitate, cujus principium, radix et origo indefectibilis est beati Petri Apostolorum Principis ejusque in Cathedra Romana Successorum suprema auctoritas et potior principalitas. Nec alia est Ecclesia Catholica nisi quae super unum Petrum aedificata in unum connexum corpus atque compactum unitate fidei et caritatis assurgit: quod beatus Cyprianus in ep. xlv. sincere professus est, dum Cornelium Papam in hunc modum alloquebatur: *ut Te collegae nostri et communionem tuam, id est Catholicae Ecclesiae unitatem pariter et caritatem, probarent firmiter ac tenerent.* Et idipsum quoque Hormisdas Pontifex ab Episcopis Acacianum schisma ejurantibus assertum voluit in formula totius christianae antiquitatis suffragio comprobata, ubi *sequestrati a communione Ecclesiae catholicae* ii dicuntur, qui sunt *non consentientes in omnibus Sedi Apostolicae.* Et tantum abest quin communiones a Romana Sede separatae jure suo catholicae nominari et haberi possint, ut potius ex hac ipsa separatione et discordia dignoscatur quaenam societates et quinam Christiani nec veram fidem teneant nec veram Christi doctrinam: quemadmodum jam inde a secundo Ecclesiae saeculo luculentissime demonstrabat S. Irenaeus lib. iii. contra Haeres. c. iii. Caveant igitur summo studio Christifideles ne hisce societatibus conjungantur, quibus salva fidei integritate nequeunt adhaerere; et audiant sanctum Augustinum docentem, nec veritatem nec pietatem esse posse ubi christiana unitas et Sancti Spiritus caritas deest.

Praeterea inde quoque a Londinensi Societate fideles abhorrere summopere debent, quod conspirantes in eam et *indifferentismo* favent et scandalum ingerunt. Societas illa, vel saltem ejusdem conditores et rectores profitentur, Photianismum et Anglicanismum duas esse ejusdem verae christianae religionis formas, in quibus aeque ac in Ecclesia Catholica Deo placere datum sit: et dissensionibus utique christianas hujusmodi communiones invicem urgeri, sed citra fidei violationem, propterea quia una eademque manet earumdem fides. Haec tamen est summa pestilentissimae indifferentiae in negotio religionis, quae hac potissimum aetate in maximam serpit animarum perniciem. Quare non est cur demonstretur Catholicos huic Societati adhaerentes spiritualis ruinae catholicis juxta atque acatholicis occasionem praebere, praesertim quum ex vana expectatione ut tres memoratae communiones integrae et in sua quaeque persuasione persistentes simul in unum coeant, Societas illa acatholicorum conversiones ad fidem aversetur et per ephemerides a se evulgatas impedire conetur.

Maxima igitur sollicitudine curandum est, ne Catholici vel specie pietatis vel mala sententia decepti Societati, de qua hic habitus est sermo, aliisque similibus adscribantur vel quoquomodo faveant, et ne fallaci novae christianae unitatis desiderio abrepti ab ea desciscant unitate perfecta, quae mirabili munere gratiae Dei in Petri soliditate consistit.

C. CARD. PATRIZI.

Romae, hac die 16 Septembris, 1864.

V.

Eminentissimo et Reverendissimo in Christo Patri et Domino C. Cardinali Patrizi, S. Officii Praeposito.

Eminentissime Domine,—

Nos infrascripti Decani, Canonici, Parochi, aliique Sacerdotes, Ecclesiae Anglo-Catholicae, Reunionem, juxta Christi voluntatem, Visibilem inter omnes partes Familiae Christianae vehementer desiderantes, Litteras ab Eminentiâ Tuâ 'Ad omnes Angliae Episcopos' emissas magno moerore perlegimus.

In his litteris Societas nostra, ad Reunionem totius Christianitatis promovendam instituta, inculpatur, quod in programmate suo ' Tres communiones, scilicet Romano-Catholicam, Orientalem atque Anglicanam, *aequo jure* Catholicum nomen sibi vindicare' affirmet.

De quâ quaestione nullam prorsus programma nostrum tulit sententiam. Quod diximus quaestionem *facti* non *juris* tractavit, affirmavimus solummodo, Ecclesiam Anglicanam nomen sibi Catholicum vindicare; quod omnibus, tam a Liturgiâ quam ab Articulis Religionis, abunde patet.

Quin etiam, quod ad Societatis nostrae intentionem attinet, in hisce litteris asseritur, nos hoc potissimum agere, ' ut tres memoratae communiones integrae, et in suâ quaeque persuasione persistentes, simul in unum coeant.'

Longe à nobis et à Societate nostrâ tale propositum absit, ex quo non unitas ecclesiastica, sed discordia fratrum sub eodem tecto comminus pugnantium, foret speranda.

Id quod a Deo O. M. enixe rogamus, quod toto corde desideramus, non aliud est, quam illa, quae ante Orientis et Occidentis scissionem, intercommunio oecumenica extitit, unius ejusdemque Fidei Catholicae professione stabilita atque compacta. Societas immo illa supra dicta eo minorem invidiam apud vos movere debet, quod, ab agendo abstinens, solummodo oret, ut, secundum Domini nostri Christi verba, ' Unus Pastor fiat, et unum Ovile.' Hoc tantum in votis nostris collocatur, et hanc sententiam et desiderium Eminentiae Tuae corde sincero et voce non fictâ pro virili parte profitemur.

Quod ad ephemeridem, cui tutulus '*The Union Review*' attinet, inter eam et Societatem nostram non nisi fortuita conjunctio exstat, ideoque nullo modo ejus dictis obligamur. In isto quidem opusculo varii scriptores opiniones proprias emittunt, ita tamen ut ex illorum sententiis evolvendis veritas Fidei Catholicae magis eluceat. Talem conscribendi rationem Romae, ubi controversiae hodiernae raro agitantur, in usu non esse vix mirandum est; at in Angliâ, ubi omnis fere quaestio fit publici juris, nulla sine liberâ disputatione in convictionem feliciter evadit.

Nos, ut in hunc eventum festinetur, multos jam annos laboravimus. Si quid minus perfectum fuerit in fide gregis, in cultu, et in disciplina cleri, nos ultra spem in melius redegimus; et, ne aliorum obliti haberemur, erga venerabilem Romae ecclesiam eâ benevolentiâ, quae apud nonnullos olim nos suspectos fecit, usi sumus.

Eminentiae tuae nos servos, Catholicae Unitatis studiosos, humiliter profitemur.

VI.

HONORABILES ET DILECTISSIMI DOMINI,

Quod vos, litteris ad me datis, *corde sincero et voce non ficta* hoc tantum optare profiteamini, ut secundum Domini Nostri Jesu Christi verba unum ovile fiat et unus pastor, id spem affert huic Sacræ Congregationi jucundissimam, vos tandem divina ejusdem Jesu Christi gratia ad veram unitatem esse perventuros. Cavendum tamen vobis est, ne ipsam quaerentes deflectatis a via. Id porro Sacra Congregatio vobis contigisse vehementer dolet existimantibus, ad veram Jesu Christi Ecclesiam pertinere, tamquam partes, Christianos illos coetus, qui *sacerdotii et catholici nominis haereditatem* habere se jactant, licet sint ab Apostolica Petri Sede divisi ac separati. Qua opinione nihil est, quod magis a genuina catholicae Ecclesiae notione abhorreat. Catholica enim Ecclesia, ut in meis ad Episcopos Angliae litteris monetur, ea est quae super unum Petrum aedificata in unum connexum corpus atque compactum unitate fidei et caritatis assurgit.* Equidem hanc fidei et caritatis seu communionis unitatem, ex irreformabili Christi institutione, non modo praecipuam esse ac fundamentalem verae Ecclesiae proprietatem, sed certissimam quoque semperque visibilem notam, qua ipsa Ecclesia ab omnibus sectis tuto ac facile distinguatur, evidentissime vobis, si rem sedulo inspicere pacatoque animo considerare volueritis, demonstrabunt tum Sacrarum Scripturarum diserta testimonia insignesque metaphorae, parabolae et imagines, quibus delineatur ac veluti repraesentatur Ecclesia, tum praeclarissima sanctorum Patrum antiquissimarumque synodorum documenta, tum constans agendi ratio, quam Ecclesia a suis usque primordiis sequi consuevit adversus cujusque generis haereticos et schismaticos, tametsi ex iis complures sacerdotii et catholici nominis haereditatem sibi arrogarent. Quemadmodum igitur Ecclesia Christi propter summam, quam per omnes gentes et in omne tempus diffusa firmissime retinet, fidei communionisque unitatem, catholica est et dicitur, ita propter unitatem eamdem sancta et apostolica praedicatur; et quemadmodum absque tali unitate desineret et jure et facto esse catholica, ita sanctitatis etiam et apostolicae successionis insignibus continuo privaretur.

At Christi Ecclesia suam unitatem nunquam amisit, nunquam ne brevissimo quidem temporis intervallo

---

* S. Ambros. de Offic. Ministr. lib. iii. c. 3, n. 19.

amittet; quippe quae perenniter, juxta divina oracula, duratura sit. Quomodo vero Ecclesia perenniter duratura credatur, si in essentialem ejus statum aetas aetati succedens, non secus atque fit in mundanarum rerum mutabilitate, novam induceret speciem et formam, et ipsa adeo Ecclesia ab illa fidei et communionis unitate desciscere aliquando posset, qua et a Jesu Christo fundata est et ab Apostolis deinde propagata? Ideo enim, ait S. Ambrosius, regnum Ecclesiae manebit in aeternum, quia individua fides, corpus est unum.* Quod si Ecclesia Christi indefectibilis prorsus est, sponte sequitur, eam infallibilem quoque dici et credi debere in evangelica doctrina tradenda; quam infallibilitatis praerogativam Christum Dominum Ecclesiae suae, cujus ipse est caput, sponsus et lapis angularis, mirabili munere contulisse, inconcussum est catholicae fidei dogma. Et profecto quis sanus sibi persuadeat, errorem subesse posse publico ac sollemni Ecclesiae magisterio, quod Christus eo consilio instituit, ut jam non simus parvuli fluctuantes et circumferamur omni vento doctrinae in nequitia hominum, in astutia ad circumventionem erroris;† quod sui praesentia nunquam deserendum, atque a Spiritu Sancto de omni veritate edocendum pollicitus est; a quo voluit universas gentes ad obedientiam fidei vocari, et rerum credendarum agendarumque doctrinam ita accipere, ut qui Apostolis legitimisque eorum successoribus praedi-

* In Luc. lib. vii. n. 91.
† Ephes. iv. 14.

cantibus non credidisset, condemnaretur ; cui munus auctoritatemque attribuit sanorum verborum formae praescribendae, in qua omnes docibiles Dei convenirent ? Hinc Paulus Ecclesiam appellat columnam et firmamentum veritatis.* Sed quo pacto Ecclesia esset firmamentum veritatis, nisi tuto ab ea veritas peteretur ? Sanctissimi quoque Patres una voce loquuntur ac praedicant, in unitate Ecclesiae unitatem fidei ac doctrinae Christi sic defixam esse ut una disjungi ab alia non valeat ; quo spectat aurea illa S. Cypriani sententia, Ecclesiam esse unitatis ac veritatis domicilium.† Neque Catholica Ecclesia dubitavit unquam de hac praerogativa sibi promissa et per jugem Christi praesentiam Sanctique Spiritus afflatum communicata, quoties subortas fidei controversias dirimere, sacrarum Scripturarum sensum interpretari, erroresque commisso revelationis deposito adversos profligare aggressa est; suas enim dogmaticas definitiones edidit semper ac proposuit tamquam certam et immutabilem fidei regulam ; quibus, ut fidei regulae, intimum quisque assensum sine ulla dubitatione, suspicione, haesitatione praestare deberet ; qui vero iisdem definitionibus contumaciter obsisterent, hoc ipso circa fidem saluti consequendae necessariam naufragavisse nec amplius ad Christi ovile pertinere censerentur. Atque haec magis magisque absurditatem produnt illius commenti de Catholica Ecclesia ex tribus communionibus

---
* 1 Timoth. iii. 15.
† Epist. viii. ad Corn. ap. Coustant, n. 1.

coalescente, cujus commenti fautores infallibilitatem Ecclesiae necessario inficiari coguntur.

Jam non minus certum atque exploratum est, Christum Jesum, ut fidei communionisque unitas in Ecclesia gigneretur ac perpetuo servaretur, utque capite constituto schismatis tolleretur occasio,* beatissimum Petrum prae caeteris Apostolis, tamquam illorum principem et ejusdem unitatis centrum et vinculum conspicuum, singulari providentia elegisse; super quem Ecclesiam suam aedificavit, et cui totius gregis pascendi, fratres confirmandi, totoque orbe ligandi ac solvendi summam curam auctoritatemque contulit in successores omni aevo prorogandam. Catholicum dogma hoc est, quod ore Christi acceptum, perenni Patrum praedicatione traditum ac defensum Ecclesia universa omni aetate sanctissime retinuit, saepiusque adversus Novatorum errores Summorum Pontificum Conciliorumque decretis confirmavit. Quare Catholica Ecclesia illa solum semper credita est, quae fide et communione cum Sede Romanorum Pontificum Petri successorum cohaeret, quam propterea Sedem S. Cyprianus nuncupat Catholicae Ecclesiae radicem et matricem;† quam unam Patres et Concilia per antonomasticam appellationem Apostolicae Sedis nomine designant; e qua sacerdotalis unitas exorta est ‡ et in omnes venerandae communionis jura dimanant;§ in qua Petrus jugiter

* S. Hieronym. lib. i. adv. Jovin. n. 26.
† Epist. iv. ad Cornelium ap. Coustant, n. 3.
‡ S. Cypr. epist. xii. ad Corn. ap. Coustant, n. 14.
§ Epist. Concilii Aquileiensis ad Gratianum Imp. an. 381, inter Epistolas S. Ambrosii.

vivit et praesidet et praestat quaerentibus fidei veritatem.* Certe S. Augustinus, ut schismatis convictos Donatistas ad radicem et vitem, unde discesserant, revocaret, argumento utitur ab antiquioribus Patribus frequentato: Venite, fratres, si vultis ut inseramini in vite. Dolor est, cum vos videmus praecisos ita jacere. Numerate sacerdotes vel ab ipsa Petri Sede, et in ordine illo patrum, quis cui successit, videte. Ipsa est petra, quam non vincunt superbae inferorum portae.† Quo uno satis ostendit, in Catholica Ecclesia eum non esse qui non inhaereat illi Petrae, in qua fundamentum positum est unitatis catholicae. Neque aliter sensit S. Hieronymus, cui profanus erat quisquis non Cathedrae Petri et Pontifici in ea sedenti communione consociaretur: Nullum primum (sic ille ad Damasum) nisi Christum sequens, beatitudini tuae, id est cathedrae Petri communione consocior; super illam petram aedificatam esse Ecclesiam scio. Quicumque extra hanc domum agnum comederit, profanus est. Si quis in Noe arca non fuerit, peribit regnante diluvio. Quicumque tecum non colligit, spargit, hoc est, qui Christi non est, Antichristi est.‡ Neque aliter S. Optatus Milevitanus, qui singularem illam cathedram celebrat, omnibus notam, Romae constitutam, in qua unitas ab omnibus ita servari debet, ut schismaticus et

---

* S. Petrus Chrysol. Epist. ad Eutych. Act. iii. Concilii Ephes. ap. Harduin, i. 1478.

† Psalm. in part. Donati.

‡ Epist. xiv. al. 57, ad Damas. n. 2.

haereticus sit, qui contra illam singularem cathedram aliam collocet.* Et merito quidem; in Romanorum enim Pontificum ordinatione et successione, uti denunciat aperte omnibus S. Irenaeus, ea quae est ab Apostolis in Ecclesia traditio et veritatis praeconatio pervenit usque ad nos; et est plenissima haec ostensio, unam et eamdem vivificatricem fidem esse quae in Ecclesia ab Apostolis usque nunc sit conservata et tradita in veritate.†

Itaque si proprium est ac perpetuum verae Christi Ecclesiae insigne, ut summa fidei caritatisque socialis unitate contineatur, efflorescat ac veluti civitas supra montem posita omnibus hominibus omni tempore patefiat; et si, alia ex parte, ejusdem unitatis originem, centrum ac vinculum Christus esse voluit Apostolicam Petri Sedem, consequens fit, coetus prorsus omnes ab externa visibilique communione et obedientia Romani Pontificis separatos, esse non posse Ecclesiam Christi, neque ad Ecclesiam Christi quomodolibet pertinere, ad illam scilicet Ecclesiam, quae in symbolo post Trinitatis commendationem credenda proponitur Ecclesia sancta, Ecclesia una, Ecclesia vera, Ecclesia catholica;‡ quae catholica nominatur non solum a suis, verum etiam ab omnibus inimicis,§ sicque ipsum catholicae nomen sola obtinuit, ut cum omnes haeretici se catholicos dici velint, quaerenti

---

* De Schism. Donatist. lib. ii. n. 2.
† Lib. iii. contra Hæres. cap. iii. n. 3, ex vet. interpr.
‡ S. Aug. de Symb. ad Catech. cap. vi.
§ S. Aug. de Vera Relig. cap. vii.

tamen peregrino alicui, ubi ad catholicam conveniatur, nullus haereticorum vel basilicam suam vel domum audeat ostendere;* per quam Christus veluti per corpus sibi penitissime conjunctum beneficia redemptionis impertit, et a qua quisque fuerit separatus, quantumlibet laudabiliter se vivere existimet, hoc solo scelere quod a Christi unitate disjunctus est, non habebit vitam, sed ira Dei manet super eum: † ejusmodi proinde coetibus catholicum nomen tum jure minime competere, tum facto attribui nullatenus posse citra manifestam haeresim. Inde autem perspicietis, honorabiles ac dilectissimi Domini, quare sacra haec Congregatio tanta sollicitudine caverit, ne Christifideles societati a vobis recens institutae ad promovendam, ut dicitis, christianitatis unitatem cooptari paterentur aut quoquomodo faverent. Perspicietis etiam in irritum necessario cadere quamcumque conciliandae concordiae molitionem, nisi ad ea principia exigatur, quibus Ecclesia et ab initio est a Christo stabilita et deinceps omni consequenti aetate per Apostolos eorumque successores una eademque in universum orbem propagata; quaeque in celeberrima Hormisdae formula, quam certum est a tota catholica Ecclesia comprobatam esse, dilucide exponuntur. Perspicietis denique, oecumenicam illam quam memoratis, *intercommunionem* ante schisma Photianum, ideo viguisse quia orientales ecclesiae nondum a de-

---

* S. Aug. contr. Epist. Fundam. cap. iv. n. 5.
† S. Aug. ep. cxli. al. 152, n. 5.

bito Apostolicae Cathedrae obsequio desciverant; neque ad optatissimam hanc intercommunionem restaurandam satis esse, simultates et odia in Romanam Ecclesiam deponere, sed omnino, ex praecepto et instituto Christi, oportere Romanae Ecclesiae fidem et communionem amplecti; quandoquidem, ut ait venerabilis Beda splendidissimum vestrae gentis ornamentum: Quicumque ab unitate fidei vel societate illius (beati Petri) quolibet modo semetipsos segregant, tales nec vinculis peccatorum absolvi nec januam possint regni caelestis ingredi.*

Atque utinam, honorabiles et dilectissimi Domini, quoniam *Ecclesia catholica una esse nec scindi nec dividi posse monstrata est*,† non amplius dubitetis, vos ejusdem Ecclesiae condere gremio, quae usque ad confessionem generis humani ab Apostolica Sede per successiones episcoporum, frustra haereticis circumlatrantibus, culmen auctoritatis obtinuit.‡ Utinam quod in vobis per inditam benevolentiam erga hanc Ecclesiam Spiritus Sanctus coepit, ipse complere et perficere sine mora dignetur. Id vobis una cum hac Sacra Congregatione toto ominatur animo et a Deo misericordiarum et luminum Patre enixe adprecatur sanctissimus Dominus Noster Pius Papa IX., ut vos tandem omnes ab exhaeredata praecisione fugientes in haereditatem Christi, in veram Catholicam Eccle-

---

* Hom. in Nat. SS. Petri et Paulli.
† S. Cypr. ep. viii. ad Corn. apud Coustant, n. 2.
‡ S. Aug. de Util. Credendi, c. xvii. n. 35.

siam, ad quam certe spectarunt majores vestri ante lugendam saeculi sextidecimi separationem, accipere feliciter mereamini radicem caritatis in vinculo pacis et in societate unitatis.* Valete.

C. CARD. PATRIZI.

Romae, hac die 8 Novembris, 1865.

* S. Aug. ep. lxi. al. 223, n. 2; ep. lxix. al. 238, n. 1.

LONDON
PRINTED BY SPOTTISWOODE AND CO
NEW-STREET SQUARE

www.ingramcontent.com/pod-product-compliance
Lightning Source LLC
Chambersburg PA
CBHW020129170426
43199CB00010B/699